HATEMONGERS
AND
DEMAGOGUES

HATEMONGERS

AND
DEMAGOGUES

Thomas Streissguth

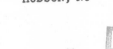

The Oliver Press, Inc.
Minneapolis

The Oliver Press, Inc.
Charlotte Square
5707 West 36th Street
Minneapolis, MN 55416-2510

Library of Congress Cataloging-in-Publication Data

Streissguth, Thomas, 1958-
Hatemongers and demagogues / Thomas Streissguth.
p.   cm.
Includes bibliographical references and index.
ISBN 1-881508-23-4
1. United States—Biography—Juvenile literature. 2. Prejudices—
United States—History—Juvenile literature. 3. Paranoia—United
States—History—Juvenile literature. 4. Racism—United States—
History—Juvenile literature. [1. United States—Biography.
2. Prejudices. 3. Paranoia. 4. Racism.] I. Title.
E176.S89   1995
920.073—dc20
[B]   94-45622
                                                 CIP
                                                  AC

ISBN: 1-881508-23-4
Profiles XVIII
Printed in the United States of America

99 98 97 96 95   8 7 6 5 4 3 2 1

Contents

For centuries, people have come to the United States in search of tolerance—but hate groups such as the Ku Klux Klan have threatened and sometimes even murdered those whose religious or racial backgrounds differed from their own.

Introduction

*H*istory is filled with admirable heroes, noble deeds, and inspiring events. Many of these events are about the struggle for freedom and the fight for equality. But there are disturbing tales as well. America has often been the scene of conflict and deceit, especially during times of economic depression or war. Many people have used tension among different groups to obtain power, riches, and fame. Claiming to be honest and dedicated to their ideals, these people have instead resorted to lies and half-truths to instil fear and suspicion in their followers. These *demagogues* often accused their enemies of belonging to an unpopular group—whether this was true or not.

In North America, the history of *hatemongering*—spreading hostility among people—can be traced back to colonial times, when Samuel Parris attacked his foes by charging them with practicing witchcraft. During the early years of the United States, Puritan minister Lyman Beecher and lawyer Thomas Watson used their influence to spread prejudice against people who did not share their religious and political views.

Ever since slavery in the U.S. came to an end following the Civil War, Ku Klux Klan leaders such as William Simmons have used violence to keep blacks out of white society. Racism in the mid-1900s also gave rise to George Lincoln Rockwell and his American Nazi Party, which was inspired by the anti-Semitic teachings of Adolf Hitler.

During the Great Depression, millions of radio listeners tuned in every week to hear Roman Catholic priest Father Charles Coughlin rail against Jews, Communists,

German dictator Adolf Hitler (1889-1945), probably the most feared hatemonger of the twentieth century, caused the deaths of six million Jewish people during the Nazi era (1933-1945).

bankers, and politicians. Some historians have compared Coughlin to Reverend Louis Farrakhan, a religious leader of the 1990s who has often distorted the truth to his Black Muslim followers to encourage racial separation.

Senator Joseph McCarthy—perhaps the most famous demagogue in U.S. history—caused a national panic in the 1950s when he accused numerous politicians and entertainers of being members of the Communist Party and, therefore, enemies of the United States.

All of these men distorted facts or invented history to make their points and win over new followers. Repeated often enough and loudly enough, their versions of events became widely accepted. Instead of working to promote tolerance, they intensified existing fears among groups.

Lessons can be learned from studying the lives of hatemongers and demagogues. In time, many of their supporters abandoned them or turned against them. The tide of resentment each rode to fame eventually gave way, leaving most of them alone and disgraced. Their hateful ideals became a thing of the past, a topic of history. But history often repeats itself. Hate can be a strong and fearsome weapon, and there will always be some people ready to take advantage of the fears of others.

*The Reverend Samuel Parris (1653-1720), one of
the key instigators of the Salem Witch Trials, told his
congregation that the Devil was at work in their town.*

1

Samuel Parris
A Witch-Hunter in Salem

*T*he time was the late 1680s, and the people of Salem in the Massachusetts Bay Colony were struggling against harsh winters, attacks from native Indian tribes, and deadly diseases. Their harvests were poor, and their supply of food and firewood was low. Because of these physical hardships, the sense of peace that religion could provide became especially important to them. Every Sunday, the villagers traveled as far as 12 miles away to attend the nearest church service. Because the journey was so long, the people of Salem village decided to establish their own congregation. In 1674, they built a new meeting house, where the congregation met for sermons and prayer. They employed several ministers before hiring the Reverend Samuel Parris in 1688.

Reverend Parris was born in London, England, in 1653 and studied at Harvard College in Cambridge as a young man. Harvard, the first college to be founded in Great Britain's North American colonies, prepared young Massachusetts men for the ministry. But Parris left Harvard after the death of his father, Thomas Parris, in 1673.

In his will, Thomas Parris had left his son the family's sugar cane plantation on Barbados, an island in the Caribbean. Samuel traveled to Barbados to run the plantation. But sugar prices were falling, and Parris soon discovered that growing and selling sugar was a difficult way to earn a living. After a hurricane damaged Parris's small plantation in 1675, he sold it. Five years later, Parris returned to Boston, where he started a trading business near the city's waterfront. Buying and selling goods from the Caribbean and Africa, he earned enough money to support his wife and daughter, and to keep a small staff of Caribbean servants.

Although Parris was hard-working and ambitious, he was unable to equal the success of his business rivals in Boston. Knowing that a successful minister could earn a comfortable living, as well as the respect of his friends and neighbors, Parris finally decided to turn to the ministry.

He searched Boston and the Massachusetts Bay Colony for a congregation that would reward him for his energy and his talent for public speaking.

The Puritans, a very strict sect of Protestants from England, had founded the colony during the 1630s. The Puritans aspired to live humbly and without sin, and they were accustomed to strict teachings. They strived to achieve a pure life dedicated to worship, and their beliefs governed all areas of their lives—from eating to business transactions to recreation. Because they were trying to create a perfect, holy society, they considered all outsiders and nonbelievers a threat to their community. The Puritans also believed that God wanted them to struggle against the Devil and the Devil's wicked followers on earth. They expected their ministers to lead them in this battle.

In 1688, the people of Salem village asked Samuel Parris to be the minister of their church. Before accepting this position, however, Parris made three important demands. He must have 1) enough pork, wheat, corn, rye, butter, and beef to feed his household; 2) free firewood, which would be cut and delivered to his home by the villagers; and 3) ownership of the ministry house and the land that surrounded it.

Parris was disappointed when the villagers could not meet his demands. They gave him only the house and the land—as well as what Parris considered a "miserly" salary. Since Parris needed a job, he accepted the offer.

Although he was dissatisfied with the bargain, some of the villagers thought Parris was getting too much. Previous ministers had only been allowed to use the ministry house—not own it.

The villagers soon found they had hired a man of strong opinions and firm beliefs. Parris insisted on strict Puritan doctrine. He detested the members of other faiths, especially Roman Catholics, and he would oppose people who questioned his teachings by denouncing them from his church pulpit. To join the congregation, villagers had to make a public declaration of their faith—men in a spoken announcement, women in writing.

Although Salem village appeared calm in this early drawing, the town would symbolize narrow-mindedness and paranoia for centuries to come.

By late 1691, Parris was growing angry with the villagers' disobedience and disrespect. Attendance at his Sunday sermons was dropping. Those who did attend often whispered or gossiped in church, or even fell asleep during services. Parris reasoned that evil forces were attacking the church and that the Devil was working to corrupt the Puritan congregation in Salem village.

Then, strange incidents began happening. Parris's 9-year-old daughter, Elizabeth, and his 11-year-old niece, Abigail Williams, began to suffer strange "fits," or seizures. For no apparent reason, their limbs would grow stiff, their voices would turn into deep growls, and their bodies would twist and fall to the floor. Invisible forces seemed to bite and pinch them as they screamed in terror. After several minutes, the fits would stop.

Parris asked a local physician, Dr. William Griggs, to examine the girls. Finding no medical reason for the convulsions, Griggs declared that the girls must be the victims of witchcraft. "The evil hand is on them," Griggs explained. Both Parris and his family accepted the doctor's diagnosis that supernatural powers were at work. When two women in Salem village, Ann Putnam and Mercy Lewis, began having similar seizures, Parris became convinced that some of his neighbors were working for the Devil and casting wicked spells.

Accusations of witchcraft had been common among Europeans for centuries. As early as the 1300s, people—especially women—were put on trial and sometimes executed for practicing black magic. European immigrants brought this belief with them to the North American colonies. In 1648, Margarate Jones of Plymouth, Massachusetts, was convicted and hanged for having a "malignant touch" that her neighbors believed could make people sick.

Parris believed that a wider conspiracy was at work in Salem village. He invited ministers from surrounding towns to come to his church and fight the Devil through fasting and prayer. Despite their efforts, Parris's daughter and niece continued to have fits and speak in a strange, incomprehensible babble.

The girls eventually blamed Tituba, Parris's servant from the West Indies, for the strange happenings. They claimed Tituba had cast a magic spell on them and had brought the Devil into their home. (Tituba had, in fact, shown the girls a form of fortunetelling that African slaves commonly practiced in the Caribbean.)

By this time, several more women in Salem village were also having seizures, including Elizabeth Hubbard, Mary Walcott, and Mary Warren. Parris demanded that Tituba explain these occurrences. When Tituba denied casting any spells, Parris beat her until she confessed to practicing witchcraft in the house. She also claimed to have seen *familiars*—wicked animals that tormented the members of the congregation at the behest of witches.

The village authorities arrested Sarah Good and Sarah Osburn (spelled *Osburne* in some records), with whom Tituba had said she had flown on a broomstick to a meeting of witches and monsters. The women were placed before a panel of *magistrates*, or judges. Already convinced that the accused were guilty of practicing witchcraft, the leading magistrate demanded their full confessions.

During the questioning, Elizabeth Parris and Abigail Williams again began having fits. They claimed that Sarah Good and Sarah Osburn were attacking them with their *specters*—ghost-like images of the women that only the tormented girls could see. Finding no other explanation for these outbursts, the magistrates were convinced that the girls were telling the truth.

Guilt or innocence in this case rested on one simple question: Had these women actually given permission for the Devil to use their invisible specters to work his mischief? On the urging of Samuel Parris and several others, the magistrates decided to accept this "spectral evidence" as proof of their guilt. On the testimony of Elizabeth Parris and Abigail Williams, the magistrates found Good and Osburn guilty of practicing witchcraft.

By the end of March 1692, more than ten young women and girls were suffering from similar fits. And all of them were naming the names of their tormentors. Finally, in May 1692, Massachusetts governor William Phips decided to convene a special court to pass judgment on anyone accused of practicing witchcraft.

Not everybody in Salem village agreed with Samuel Parris and the magistrates. Martha Corey, one of the women suspected of practicing witchcraft, ridiculed the proceedings. She claimed that witches and witchcraft did not exist. Her husband, Giles, said the court was acting irresponsibly and pointed out that the women might be lying. The court officials then accused him, too, of witchcraft.

Most of the villagers did not listen to the Coreys' arguments. The hunt for witches had put a great fear of

As more people experienced "fits" or outbursts during the witch trials in Salem, many others became convinced that evil spirits were attacking the village.

the supernatural into them. Ready at the smallest sign or suspicion to find witches among their neighbors, the villagers used gossip, rumors, and false accusations to discredit others. Samuel Parris, too, used this mass hysteria to his advantage. In his Sunday sermons, Parris blamed the troubles on the sins of the villagers, who had brought the Devil into town by neglecting their spiritual duties to the church.

The people living in the British colonies had seen witchcraft cases before. Several of these cases had resulted in executions. Often, someone would accuse an outcast—someone who was homeless or unsociable—of being a witch. Unmarried, older women who lived alone were often under suspicion, as were people who did not attend church. Accusers sometimes used the charge of witchcraft against someone they disliked. Or they would accuse someone with whom they had fought over land or debts.

Usually, an accused person was tried privately in court and then cast out from the community. Samuel Parris and the judges involved in the Salem case, however, chose a different course by holding public hearings.

As news of witchcraft in Salem spread to neighboring towns, an increasing number of people began making charges. Before the end of summer in 1692, the people of the Massachusetts Bay Colony had accused more than 200 people of witchcraft. Some of the accused were prominent and well-respected citizens, such as Governor Phips's wife.

The Salem witches were executed on the authority of a biblical passage, Exodus 22:18, "Thou shalt not suffer a witch to live." The first victim of the special court was Bridget Bishop, who was found guilty on June 2, 1692, and hanged eight days later. Though well-liked and respected, 71-year-old Rebecca Nurse died on the gallows on July 19 with four other women, including Sarah Good. Five more people were executed on August 19.

Because he refused to enter a plea before the magistrates, Giles Corey was ordered to be pressed with heavy stones until he confessed. The sentence was carried out on September 19. But instead of confessing, Corey only said "more weight." He died during the torture. Eight more people were hanged on September 22, including Martha Corey. In all, the special court put 20 men and women to death during the summer and autumn of 1692. Two prisoners also died in jail, one of whom was Sarah Osburn.

Throughout this time, Samuel Parris ranted and raved against the witches and encouraged his congregation to join his crusade against the Devil. He quoted from the biblical verse of John 6:70, in which Jesus Christ accuses one of his disciples of acting like the Devil.

Around the time of Giles Corey's death, a fear grew among the people of Salem village that they were doing wrong. Many of those people accused of witchcraft were showing great courage and faith on their way to the gallows. Others were confessing to avoid punishment, even

Throughout history, many people have used the words of Jesus Christ and other religious leaders to justify violence and intolerance.

though the court had little evidence against them. Some people were still uncertain about spectral evidence, about the young girls who were making accusations, and about Samuel Parris's claims that the region was under attack by the Devil.

Many members of the congregation came to believe that innocent people were being put to death, although Parris told them otherwise. Even some of the magistrates were beginning to doubt the testimony they heard in the courtroom. Robert Pike, a magistrate from the nearby town of Salisbury, claimed that the Devil was using the Salem court proceedings to harm innocent people.

21

Two villagers suspected of witchcraft are held in stocks awaiting their executions.

Nathaniel Saltonstall, another magistrate, decided to withdraw from the court in protest.

Even Puritan leaders began to criticize the proceedings. Increase Mather, a prominent minister and the president of Harvard University, publicly condemned the trials. In his 1693 book, *Cases of Conscience Concerning Evil Spirits*, Mather wrote that the Devil sometimes brought confusion and panic to good Christians. Although Mather claimed that the Salem magistrates had acted legally, he also urged that the special court be ended. The opinions of Increase Mather carried great weight among the Puritans in the Massachusetts Bay Colony. His book gave Governor Phips enough authority and support to put an end to the special court. Phips quickly did so.

At the same time, Samuel Parris asked his congregation for reconciliation. He still blamed his opponents for the trouble in the village and stood by his belief that his congregation had been attacked by the Devil. But he also wished to stay in Salem village and keep his job and his property.

With the disbanding of the court, the witchcraft panic died down. The people of Salem, however, were not ready to forgive Parris. Many refused to attend his sermons or pay taxes for his salary. In 1695, the village called on Increase Mather and other leaders of the Massachusetts Bay Colony to help resolve the differences with their minister. Two years later, the villagers and

The Reverend Increase Mather helped to end the Salem Witch Trials, but his son (pictured here), Puritan clergyman Cotton Mather (1663-1728), strongly supported them, believing that witchcraft had caused his daughter's illness.

Parris finally made an agreement. In return for Parris's resignation, the congregation would pay Parris his unpaid salary as well as the costs of the ministry house and his property.

In 1697, Judge Samuel Sewall, who had presided over some of the witch trials, publicly admitted his shame for having been involved in the proceedings. Twenty people who had accused others of being witches signed a document stating, "We fear we have been instrumental with others, though ignorantly and unwillingly, to bring upon ourselves the guilt of innocent blood." In 1706, Ann Putnam, one of the first people in Salem village to accuse others of practicing witchcraft, would publicly state that she had lied 14 years earlier and that the Devil had tricked her into believing in witches and specters.

Before 1697 came to an end, Parris left Salem. He spent the rest of his life struggling to support his family, drifting around the colony and working as a teacher and farmer and trading in land and goods. He thought about returning to Barbados but decided against it. At one point, he even considered becoming a minister in the village of Stow (in what is now the state of Maine). But the residents of Stow and Parris could not agree on a salary or on an allowance for firewood. Parris eventually settled down on a farm in the village of Sudbury, Massachusetts, where he died in February 1720.

The belief in witchcraft would continue, but no more witches would be executed in the English colonies. Because of the events that transpired in Salem, the term *witch-hunt* is still used to describe any situation when unfounded accusations are made against the innocent, or when authorities search recklessly to find a perpetrator of a crime.

Motivated by his strong religious convictions, Lyman Beecher (1775-1863) preached that anyone with religious beliefs different from his own was a threat to the United States.

2

Lyman Beecher
The Passionate Puritan

*A*fter the American Revolution brought independence to the British colonies in the late 1700s, citizens of the new United States were free to follow the religious teachings of their choice. While the U.S. Constitution guaranteed freedom of religion, many citizens of the young nation still disliked or feared people whose beliefs or practices differed from their own.

Members of several Protestant denominations, who considered themselves to be the nation's original settlers, did not tolerate Roman Catholics, with whom they disagreed on many issues. The members of small religious groups, such as the Mennonites and Shakers, would not associate with people who did not share their views. Instead, they established isolated communities of their own on the western frontier. Despite its hard-won freedom, the nation was still divided, and violence often broke out between ethnic groups and social classes.

At this time, Lyman Beecher was growing up in Guilford, Connecticut, which had once been part of the New Haven Colony. This Puritan colony had been a *theocracy*, a state governed by religious leaders. Lyman, who was born in 1775, had a long line of Puritan ancestors, and his father and grandfather worked as blacksmiths. Because Lyman's mother died two days after his birth, Lyman's father, David Beecher, sent the newborn to live on a farm with his aunt and uncle. Hard work in the open fields and pastures of Guilford made Lyman a strong, robust young man.

Lyman decided to attend Yale College (now Yale University) in the nearby city of New Haven, Connecticut. Yale was the intellectual center of a strict religious philosophy known as Calvinism, an important foundation of Puritan beliefs. Calvinists accepted the Bible as the literal truth. They also believed in the concept of *predestination*—that God had already decided which people would go to heaven or hell after they died. People's actions on earth, whether good or bad, could not change this predestined fate.

By the time Lyman Beecher arrived at Yale during the late 1700s, new ideas were causing trouble and turmoil among the school's clergy and students. The French and British soldiers who fought in the Revolutionary War had brought new ideas to North America from Europe. Some of these soldiers were *deists*, who believed that God had stopped intervening in the world after creating the universe. Others were *atheists*, who did not believe in the existence of God at all. Many others believed that "natural laws" or the workings of chance governed the world and determined the outcome of events.

Yale became a center of the fierce debate surrounding the new ideas. The many new scientific discoveries made during this period also caused many students to

Yale College (later Yale University)—the third oldest college in the United States—was founded in 1701.

become more skeptical of strict Calvinist beliefs and of other religious doctrines.

The Calvinists, in turn, believed that the loss of religious faith was leading to a breakdown in society. A few of Yale's teachers and ministers stood firmly against the revolutionary tide of new ideas. Timothy Dwight, the president of Yale College, tried to reassure doubting students, many of whom were dropping out of school. Dwight's sermons turned many of them away from deism and back to traditional religion.

Timothy Dwight (1752-1817), the president of Yale College from 1795 to 1817, supported the idea of a theocracy, in which religious leaders would run the government.

Dwight made a great impression on Lyman Beecher. Inspired by Dwight's words and arguments, Beecher decided to enter the ministry. He gave his first sermon in the nearby town of West Haven. After graduating from Yale, Beecher studied with Dwight for another year and was soon licensed as a Calvinist minister. In 1798, Beecher left New Haven to fill a vacant ministry post in East Hampton, a small whaling village on Long Island, New York.

Samuel Buell, the former *parson* (or clergyman) of East Hampton, had preached a strict Calvinism in the town church for more than 50 years, and Beecher carried on this tradition. He spoke out against rebels and doubters and rallied his congregation to adhere to traditional Calvinist beliefs. After spending a year in East Hampton, Beecher was ordained as the town's minister. His pay was $300 a year—a generous salary at that time—plus a supply of firewood for his home.

Although Beecher was successful as a small-town minister, he was always looking for new opportunities to express his beliefs. He had strong opinions on the events of the day. He preached against the practice of dueling after Alexander Hamilton, a national political leader, was killed in a duel in 1804. (A duel is a prearranged fight with pistols or other deadly weapons between two persons—usually to settle a point of honor.) Beecher also spoke out against gambling and drinking alcohol. Fearless in any public debate, he usually overwhelmed his

31

opponents with fiery language and an unbending loyalty to his own principles. But Beecher's involvement in social issues troubled some members of his congregation in East Hampton. They believed that his rightful place was in the church and that he should stay out of worldly affairs.

Around this time, Beecher's growing number of children was putting a strain on his finances. But several

This illustration of the interior of a church during the early 1800s shows the congregation looking back to greet a latecomer.

people opposed him when he asked the town of East Hampton for a raise in salary. The congregation claimed that he was living too well and that he was taking more interest in politics and public affairs than in matters of faith. For several years, the debate dragged on while Beecher grew more and more frustrated.

In the spring of 1810, about 12 years after coming to East Hampton, Beecher resigned from his ministry. He then moved to Litchfield, Connecticut, where the towns-people hired him as their minister at a salary of $800 a year. The new minister felt at home in Connecticut, where laws had established Puritanism as the state religion and decreed that the church would be supported with public money. The church ran the public school system, and all students were required to study the Bible and attend church services regularly. (This would change in 1818, when the state legislature approved the legal separation of church and state.)

When Beecher arrived in Connecticut, few people living in the state openly challenged predestination and other Calvinist doctrines. Fewer still believed in a world governed by natural laws and the workings of chance. Beecher taught that the seemingly random events that occurred in the world were really the product of God's will. Beecher believed his mission was to introduce everyone in the United States to traditional Calvinism. He spoke out passionately against other religions and did his best to keep his congregation loyal to him.

By the mid-1820s, Litchfield had grown too small for Lyman Beecher. He was again longing for a larger and more prestigious post. This time he aimed at Boston, Massachusetts, the most challenging and controversial of all religious battlegrounds.

At that time, Boston was in the midst of a religious conflict between the Unitarians and the Congregationalists. Both of these groups had their origins in the early Puritan churches of New England. But the many rival Unitarian churches that were springing up in Boston were posing a grave threat to the established Congregationalist churches.

The Unitarians, who were increasing in number, believed that people had free will. They denied the concept of predestination and did not believe that Jesus Christ had been the Son of God. The Unitarians not only disagreed with many Puritan beliefs, they also ridiculed them. Beecher thought the Unitarians were destroying government-run institutions, such as the courts and legislatures.

Boston's Congregationalists, on the other hand, believed that Jesus Christ was the leader of their "family of God." They were looking for someone to help them in their struggle with the Unitarians, and Beecher's reputation as a strong orator prompted them to invite him to become pastor of their Hanover Street Church. When Beecher arrived in Boston in 1826, he found that he not only would have to contend with Unitarians, deists, and atheists, but would also have to face what he perceived as his most powerful enemy, the Roman Catholic Church.

Protestant groups had broken off from the Catholic Church in Europe as early as the 1500s. Over the centuries, Catholic officials had sometimes tortured and executed Protestants who would not conform to Catholic beliefs. Many Protestant groups living in the United States, including Calvinists, were afraid of what might happen if Catholic immigrants moved from Europe to the United States.

During the early 1800s, thousands of immigrants from European countries—especially Ireland and Germany—had brought their Catholic practices and beliefs with them to the United States. These immigrants made up a growing part of Boston's working class. Many people who were born in Boston or in other New England cities—and who may have forgotten that their own ancestors had been immigrants—often viewed these newcomers as a threat to the nation. When Lyman Beecher arrived in Boston, many anti-Catholics had already begun to fight back with threats and violence.

Beecher soon became a leader of the growing anti-immigration movement. His thundering sermons against the sins of the Catholic Church helped to earn him the nickname "Brimstone Beecher." He stoked the fires of religious, ethnic, and class hatred in Boston with his anti-Catholic oratory and a voice that could overpower a church organ.

35

Although the United States had essentially been founded by immigrants, many Americans during the 1800s worried about the influence that new groups of immigrants would have on the political and religious future of the nation.

Beecher and many of his followers believed that the pope, the leader of the world's Roman Catholics, was plotting against Protestants and the government of the United States. Beecher also believed that Catholic immigrants had come to Boston to turn the United States into a Roman Catholic nation. He thought these immigrants were poor, lazy, and dangerous drunkards who would place a great burden on the city with their large families. These immigrants, he preached, were a threat to the livelihood of Protestant workers—who often called themselves "native" Americans, since they had been born in the United States.

Beecher's sermons moved and inspired his listeners. His words may have prompted the wave of "nativist" violence against immigrants in the city. In 1829, a bloody anti-Catholic riot in Boston lasted for three days and caused many deaths and injuries.

By the 1830s, anti-Catholicism was spreading throughout New England. Protestant magazines attacked the Catholics, falsely accusing their priests of abducting and murdering innocent children. Many people thought that Catholic monks were depraved and that Catholic nuns were immoral. Politicians began using the threat of a Catholic takeover of the government in their campaigns for office. To raise donations in small towns and large cities, traveling Protestant ministers spread the word of the Catholic menace.

Beecher rode this wave of anti-Catholic hatred, but the ride proved to be a rough one for him. In February 1830, arsonists burned down his Boston church. The Boston firefighters, who greatly resented Beecher's opposition to liquor and gambling, did nothing to stop the blaze. Instead, they danced and laughed as liquor casks in the church basement exploded with a rush of flame and smoke. (Beecher had allowed a local merchant to lease space and store the casks in the church, but he may not have known they contained alcohol.) The police never caught the parties responsible for the arson.

During the wave of "nativism," Protestant leaders used rumors and scandals as their weapons. According to one rumor, the Catholic Church intended to conquer the new frontier that was opening west of the Appalachian Mountains. In 1832, convinced that the frontier needed saving, Beecher accepted a new post as president of Lane Theological Seminary in Cincinnati, Ohio.

Beecher found an entirely new conflict brewing at Lane, a school that was affiliated with the Presbyterian Church (a Protestant denomination with roots in Calvinism). Antislavery students and teachers were sharply divided between the *abolitionists*, who wanted to free slaves on American soil, and the *colonizers*, who wanted to free slaves and send them to Africa.

Although Beecher was somewhat indifferent to the conflict, the students saw him as sympathetic to the colonizers. Many people living in Cincinnati, however, supported slavery and were opposed to the activities and debates among the Lane students. Some local citizens planned to organize a mob and storm the school to drive away its faculty and students.

Meanwhile, riots, fires, and street fighting between Protestants and Catholics continued throughout New England. On August 11, 1834, a crowd of Protestants attacked a Catholic school in Charlestown, Massachusetts. Believing the school's staff was forcing students to become

Heated debates in colleges were common during the early 1800s, when students from Lane Theological Seminary disagreed over the the issue of slavery.

Catholics, a Protestant mob burned down the school. Because Lyman Beecher, who had returned to the city for a visit, had criticized the Catholic school in his sermons, the Catholics of Boston placed the blame for the fire squarely on his shoulders.

While Beecher was away from Cincinnati, the trustees of the Lane seminary decided to take action and ban students from holding further debates about slavery. Although Lyman Beecher had played no part in this decision, the students now saw their college's president as a tyrant who would take away their right to free speech and debate. On October 15, 1834, more than half of

Whether slavery should be outlawed in the United States was controversial throughout the nation, as people held different economic, moral, and personal beliefs about the practice of keeping people as property.

Lane's students left the college to start a new one—Oberlin College. (Oberlin became the first college in the country to accept students of both sexes, as well as students of all races.)

Beecher's troubles, however, did not end there. Since Lane was a Presbyterian school, Beecher had accepted the doctrines of Presbyterianism, in which church leaders are elected by their congregation. A Plan of Union between the Congregational and Presbyterian churches had enabled Beecher to preach in a Presbyterian parish in East Hampton, a Congregational pulpit in Litchfield, and then again in another Presbyterian church in Boston. Although Beecher had foreseen no problems at Lane, the church put him on trial, charging him with hypocrisy and heresy in 1835. A staunch group of traditional Presbyterians did not accept a convert within their ranks and tried to have him fired.

During the 1840s, Lyman Beecher began supporting many reforms that would gain more support in the decades to come, including the temperance movement to limit drinking, the abolition movement to end slavery, and the women's suffrage movement to give women the right to vote.

Beecher was able to convince the church officials to let him stay, and he remained at Lane until the late 1840s. By then Beecher was in his mid-sixties. He no longer had enough energy to deliver his fiery sermons. After leaving Lane Seminary, Beecher moved with his large family back home to Connecticut. While nativists fought for control of state and federal legislatures, and while anti-Catholic violence swept through U.S. cities, Beecher settled into a comfortable retirement.

During the 1840s and 1850s, people who supported many of Beecher's beliefs joined secret societies and political groups that worked to stop the rising numbers of immigrants and Roman Catholics in the United States. Members of these groups were sometimes called the Know-Nothings. If strangers asked them about the movement, they would say, "I know nothing."

Meanwhile, many of Beecher's 13 children gained fame and respect that rivaled that of their father—even though their beliefs sometimes clashed with his. One of his daughters, Catherine Beecher, fought for the education of women. Henry Ward Beecher, one of his sons, preached in Brooklyn, New York, and was known for his strong views against slavery.

Harriet Beecher Stowe, another of Lyman's children, wrote *Uncle Tom's Cabin*, a best-selling antislavery novel that electrified the people of the United States when it first appeared in print in 1852. The debate over slavery would soon split the nation into two warring

Harriet Beecher Stowe (1811-1896), who drew attention to the abolition movement with her 1852 novel, Uncle Tom's Cabin, *inherited her father's ability to make impassioned, persuasive arguments.*

halves—North and South. In 1863, as the nation was in the midst of the bloody Civil War, Lyman Beecher passed away.

Although politician and journalist Thomas Watson (1856-1922) spent his early career promoting tolerance, a chain of events caused him to reconsider his views and start spreading racial and religious hatred.

3

Thomas Watson
A Reformer Turned Racist

*T*he South was an angry place in the years immediately following the Civil War. When the Thirteenth Amendment to the U.S. Constitution outlawed slavery in 1865, many southern planters who had relied on slave labor went bankrupt. Then, the federal government passed the Reconstruction Acts, which authorized the military to occupy the southern states and to organize new state governments. Many Southerners saw this as another invasion of their land.

Thomas Edward Watson witnessed these hard times while growing up on a plantation in Columbia County, Georgia. His uncle had been killed during the Civil War, and his father, John Smith Watson, had been wounded twice. Thomas was eight years old when the war ended in 1865. The 45 slaves who had worked on the Watson farm were given their freedom. Without slaves to harvest their cotton crop, the Watsons lost their land and their livelihood.

They weren't alone. As prices for their produce fell and their debts increased, farmers went hungry. Many left for the cities in search of factory work, which paid poorly. Meanwhile, businessmen from the North were coming to southern cities to profit from the rebuilding of the South. With the help of cheap labor, these northerners operated new factories, mills, and railroads. They held down the price of cotton and charged high fees to ship crops on the railroads. Hatred and resentment against these northerners and their businesses simmered among many southern farmers—including Thomas Watson.

In 1872, Watson entered Mercer University in Macon, Georgia. His father had become an alcoholic after losing the family plantation, and he often spoke before local temperance societies, which tried to limit or outlaw alcohol consumption. After graduating from college, he worked as a clerk for a local judge and got his license to practice law in 1875.

Still young and inexperienced, Watson attracted few clients and earned little money as an attorney. To get by, he had to work briefly as a school teacher and then as a farm laborer. In time, however, he began to make a name for himself in the Georgia law courts. Many of Watson's clients were poor farmers who were having trouble paying off their bank debts. Having lived through rural poverty himself, he sympathized with his clients and defended them with inspiring courtroom speeches. He blamed banks, the growing railroad industry, and big businesses for the farmers' plight. Although Watson was fighting to protect people who were otherwise defenseless, a chain of events in his life would gradually turn him into a leading voice of hatred and prejudice.

Eventually, the troubles he saw on a regular basis spurred Watson to action. He joined the Democratic Party, which claimed to represent the interests of Georgia's farmers and laborers. He also gained statewide fame after speaking at the 1880 Democratic convention. Two years later, he ran for the Georgia state legislature. During his campaign, Watson called for an end to Georgia's convict-leasing law, which allowed businesses to hire convicted criminals as laborers for very low wages. He also proposed the establishment of public schools for the state's black residents. Blacks and whites should work together, he said, to fight the big-business practices that were hurting farmers.

Voters identified with Watson and elected him to the Georgia legislature that year. As a state legislator, Watson proposed several bills to help the poor. But many Republican and Democratic politicians opposed Watson's ideas, and most of his bills were defeated in the legislature. Frustrated and angry, he resigned from the legislature in the summer of 1884, before the end of his term.

Many farmers liked Watson's ideas and continued to support him. A growing tide of anti-business sentiment rallied them to action. In the late 1880s, farmers banded together to fight for their interests and formed a new political organization known as the Farmers Alliance. By sharing the profits of their farms, Alliance members hoped to survive the hard times they were going through. Members of the Alliance supported Watson when he ran for a seat in the U.S. Congress in 1890. That November, he easily beat his Republican opponent.

In Washington, D.C., Watson ran into the same opposition he had faced in Georgia. Republicans and conservative Democrats blocked his reform measures. Convinced that the Democrats had given in to northern business interests, Watson abandoned the Democratic Party and formed a new political party—the Populist Party (also known as the People's Party). He immediately invited other dissatisfied Democrats to become Populists. Legislators from Kansas, Nebraska, and Minnesota joined him, and Watson became the leader of the nine-member Populist caucus in Congress.

The Populists called for a mandatory eight-hour workday, a national graduated income tax, a public takeover of the railroads, and the direct election of U.S. senators by voters. (At that time, senators were selected by state legislatures rather than through a popular vote.) The Populist caucus failed to pass the new policies, although many would become law in years to come. Watson did sponsor one bill that passed during his term, creating the Rural Free Delivery (RFD) of the U.S. mail.

While in Washington, Watson gained many enemies with his charges that Democratic and Republican members of Congress were corrupt. Watson's accusations brought a strong counterattack from both parties. At the same time, many Populists were being publicly criticized and physically attacked in Georgia. His opponents began to regard Watson as a dangerous rebel who wanted to return the South to a plantation economy. Anti-Populists beat and even murdered some of Watson's supporters.

During his campaign for the U.S. House of Representatives in 1892, Watson's opponent was James Black, who had the support of most Democrats and business interests. The race sparked violence between Democrats and Populists. Angry mobs fought in the streets, and Watson endured scathing attacks from the press and threats on his life.

Before the election, officials of the Democratic Party added false names to the voting lists to increase the number of votes that Black received. Party officials also stuffed ballot boxes with phony ballots, paid black people to vote for their candidate, and threatened other blacks who supported Watson. These illegal practices helped Black to win by a wide margin.

After the election, Watson grew angry at African Americans in general. Watson had once supported political equality for blacks and he had spoken out against lynchings of blacks. (Lynchings, usually carried out by a mob, are illegal hangings of people without due process of the law.) But he changed his mind because he felt black voters had betrayed him.

Although Watson had been defeated, the campaign had made him a hero to Populists around the country. And the times were right for Populist ideas. An economic panic in 1893 caused bank failures, factory closings, lower prices for agricultural products, and widespread unemployment. Many people believed the federal government had favored eastern banks and industrial leaders at the expense of farmers and laborers. The Populists wanted economic reforms to help the average person, not just wealthy businessmen. Watson's speeches in Georgia and neighboring states were drawing huge and enthusiastic crowds.

Despite his rising popularity, Watson again lost a congressional election to Black in 1894. By this time, it was clear to other city officials and the press that Black had used illegal practices to win. The congressman offered to resign temporarily from office and run against

Hundreds of African Americans were lynched during the late 1800s and early 1900s by angry whites who could not accept blacks as their equals under the law.

Watson again in a special election. Watson accepted this opportunity, but Black won the second election as well.

These two defeats made Tom Watson a bitter and angry man. But he was still a hero to the Populists, and he was still a man whom the Democrats thought might be able to win a national election. Watson was nominated by the Populist Party to join the campaign of 1896 as the candidate for vice-president of the United States. In an attempt to strengthen their party by linking it to the Democratic ticket, the Populists nominated William Jennings Bryan for president. (The Democrats had already nominated Bryan, with Arthur Sewall as his vice-presidential candidate.) Watson campaigned hard for himself and for Bryan, although Sewall would have been vice-president if Bryan won.

Bryan and Watson spoke out for a controversial policy that would allow the U.S. government to print more money. The two men hoped that the proposed policy would help farmers to earn more. But powerful officials who were closely allied with business opposed this policy and despised the Populists. They gave Watson no support, and his name did not even appear on the ballot in several states. Bryan himself disliked Watson and had little sympathy for the plight of southern farmers. Additionally, many Populists opposed Watson's alliance with the Democrats.

Populists Bryan and Watson lost on election day to Republican candidates William McKinley and Theodore Roosevelt. Divided and weakened by the campaign, the Populists were also losing their support among the voters, partly because farm prices started rising again. Watson's political career seemed to be finished.

After the campaign, Watson retired from politics. Although still committed to Populist ideas, he refused to run when the Populists of Georgia nominated him for governor in 1898. To pay his debts, he returned to his law practice and wrote a series of biographies. His subjects included men whom he considered "Populists," including U.S. presidents Thomas Jefferson and Andrew Jackson, and French leader Napoleon Bonaparte. Watson also

Democrat-Populist William Jennings Bryan (1860-1925), who ran unsuccessfully for president in 1896, 1900, and 1908, served under Democratic president Woodrow Wilson as the U.S. secretary of state from 1913 to 1915.

wrote a nostalgic novel entitled *Bethany: A Story of the Old South.*

In the early 1900s, Watson returned to public life. Still a popular figure in Georgia, he won over large crowds to his views on the evils of big business and big government. The Populist Party nominated him for president in 1904. Watson agreed to run, but he received only 117,000 votes, losing to Republican Theodore Roosevelt. Nevertheless, the nation was going through an era of reform that was spurred by Populist demands. Newspapers were describing the terrible situation in urban slums and factories, and politicians began passing laws to improve conditions for both farmers and urban workers.

These new "progressive" reformers saw Watson as one of their own. A New York editor invited Watson to start a new periodical, *Tom Watson's Magazine*, which would feature Watson's own articles and editorials, as well as articles written by prominent people of the time, such as novelist Theodore Dreiser and attorney Clarence Darrow. The first issue appeared in March 1905, and the magazine soon gained a wide circulation.

Watson was still playing a big role in Georgia politics by endorsing candidates he liked, including a Democrat named Hoke Smith, who ran for governor in 1906. To help Smith win, Watson now spoke publicly against black voting rights, and he took up the cause of *white supremacy*—the belief that the white race is superior to other races. Watson knew that most blacks at that time still voted Republican—the party of former president Abraham Lincoln, who had helped to end slavery in the United States. Watson tried to frighten voters by describing blacks as violent, rebellious, and dangerous. Many people shared Watson's opinions, and his tactics worked—a majority of Georgia voters elected Hoke Smith to office. The election also spawned a four-day race riot in Atlanta in which 10 blacks and 2 whites were killed, and another 60 black people injured.

In 1908, the Populist Party again nominated Watson for president. This time, he used white supremacy as the theme for his campaign. He spoke out against giving any further rights to blacks. Although Watson had many followers, few people were willing to support this third-party candidate when they reached the polls. He received only 30,000 votes in the presidential election that sent Republican William Howard Taft to the White House.

That same year, Watson turned on his ally Hoke Smith, who was again running for governor. Smith had angered Watson by allowing the execution of Arthur Glover, a Watson supporter who had been convicted of murder in Georgia. In his own newspaper, *Watson's Jeffersonian Magazine*, Watson wrote venomous editorials and published outrageous charges of corruption and wrongdoing against Smith. Watson gave big headlines and long stories to the slightest rumor or scandal against his enemy. As a result, Smith lost the election.

By now, many progressive readers, shocked by views they found bigoted and immoral, had abandoned Watson. *Tom Watson's Magazine* had closed down, but the *Jeffersonian* was popular in southern states, especially in Georgia. At his home at Hickory Hill, Georgia, Watson built his own printing plant and used his presses to denounce his political enemies—especially Hoke Smith—as well as corporations, industrialists, bankers, northerners, Jews, and Roman Catholics. Watson saw Catholics as a threat to the independence and liberty of the entire United States. According to Watson and many other anti-Catholics, the Catholic pope was plotting to overthrow the U.S. government. Watson maintained that

Catholic priests wanted to convert the entire population of the United States to Catholicism. But Watson especially despised blacks, calling them a "hideous, ominous national menace."

Although Watson had become a controversial figure in the United States, he still enjoyed a reputation as a superb lawyer. In 1913, Leo Frank, a pencil factory manager accused of murdering one of his employees, Mary Phagan, asked Watson to represent him in the case. Not only did Watson turn down Frank's request, but he also began writing angry accusations against Frank in his publications. Watson regarded Leo Frank, who was Jewish and from the north, as a symbol of the big-business interests that had ruined the South. Watson accused Frank's defenders of trying to corrupt the Georgia judicial system.

The jury found Frank guilty, and the judge sentenced him to death for the murder of Mary Phagan. This sentence outraged many writers and politicians, who demanded a new trial. Determined to see Frank hang, Watson made a deal with Georgia governor John Slaton. If Slaton would allow Frank to be executed, Watson would support a Slaton campaign for the U.S. Senate. Despite this promise, however, Slaton reduced Frank's sentence and allowed him to live.

In the pages of the *Jeffersonian*, Watson threatened Leo Frank with a public lynching. Watson's angry articles were filled with anti-Jewish statements and attacks against John Slaton. The *Jeffersonian* had a strong impact on public opinion. On August 16, 1915, a group of men kidnapped Frank from his jail cell, drove him 200 miles to the town of Marietta, Georgia—where Mary Phagan had been born—and hanged him from a tree limb. This act would soon inspire the founding of the modern Ku Klux Klan.

Satisfied with his work on the Frank case, Watson turned his attention to other matters. He denounced

Georgia governor John Slaton (right) refused to give in to Thomas Watson's demands to hang Leo Frank (bottom).

But Watson's hateful words prompted unknown assailants to take the law into their own hands and lynch Leo Frank.

World War I, which had begun in 1914, as a conspiracy of business interests and accused the Catholic pope of plotting with Germany against the United States. He also accused the American Legion, an organization of U.S. war veterans, of being a corrupt group of bloodthirsty murderers.

In the summer of 1917, Watson decided to bring legal action against the Conscription Act, a federal law that allowed the U.S. government to draft young men into the army. Watson argued that the draft violated the civil liberties of Americans, but he lost the case. Opposing the federal government's policies was risky during wartime, because the U.S. government was using another law—the Espionage Act—to silence critics of the war effort. In August 1917, the U.S. Post Office, convinced that Watson's publication was hurting the war effort, took away his mailing privileges. *Watson's Jeffersonian Magazine* shut down soon afterward.

In 1920, Watson decided to run once more for the Senate against his old ally and enemy, Hoke Smith. By this time, most members of the Democratic and Republican parties were strongly opposed to Watson. But Watson's strong convictions, angry speeches, and reputation as a fighter for southern causes had brought him widespread popularity in Georgia, and he won the election.

For the rest of his life, Watson continued his tirades against the military and big business. He nearly came to

VALDOSTA KLAN-OPEN AIR CEREMOI
KNIGHTS KU KLUX KLAN
VALDOSTA, GA. OCT. 10, 192

Many of Tom Watson's racist attitudes were shared by members of the Ku Klux Klan.

blows with his opponents in the Senate chamber on several occasions. Bitter and depressed over his previous failures, Watson gradually sank into alcoholism just as his father had. On September 25, 1922, he died during a severe attack of asthma and bronchitis.

Thomas Watson was buried at Hickory Hill, and 7,000 mourners attended his funeral. Although many people despised him, others praised him for his fighting spirit and his defense of the farmer and of southern traditions. One of the wreaths laid near his casket was a large cross made of red roses, sent by the Ku Klux Klan.

*During the early 1900s, William Simmons
(1880-1946) revitalized the Ku Klux Klan.*

4

William Simmons
Imperial Wizard of the Ku Klux Klan

*O*n Christmas Eve night in 1865, six men gathered in a small office in Pulaski, Tennessee. They were Confederate veterans who had fought for the South during the Civil War. The war had left their side defeated and humiliated. Their traditional way of life had ended, because the black slaves who had worked in their homes and fields were now free people. Angry and restless, these men decided to form a secret organization to win back the honor of the South. They would adopt ceremonial names, wear uniforms to hide their identities, and reclaim their sense of pride.

Late into the night, the men argued over what name to select for their new organization. They finally agreed to adopt a version of the word *kuklos* (which means "circle" in Greek) and to add the word *klan* to represent the ancient clans of Scotland, their common ancestral homeland. Thus, the Ku Klux Klan was born.

The Klansmen had to keep their society secret. In the postwar South, northern-allied businessmen and politicians controlled much of state government. The Klan was illegal, and its members risked jail terms for their activities. During its first few years of existence, the organization served primarily as a social club for members. But soon the Klan grew more dangerous.

The Klan members came out in costume at night. They rode through the countryside on horseback, disguised by sheets and pillowcases. Their disguises terrified some of the freed slaves who lived in the Tennessee countryside.

Word of the Klan spread quickly throughout Tennessee and its neighboring states. Hundreds of unemployed men and Civil War veterans took the Klan's oath and promised to fight for white supremacy. In the spring of 1866, the Klan recruited Nathan Bedford Forrest, a former commander in the Confederate army during the Civil War. Forrest, a daring cavalry leader

This illustration shows early members of the Ku Klux Klan, before the organization had a standard, all-white uniform.

Confederate general Nathan Bedford Forrest (1821-1877), one of the most glorified military leaders of the Civil War, was also one of many angry southerners who joined the Ku Klux Klan after the conflict had ended.

and former slave trader, saw the Klan as a way to carry on the fight against the North.

Klan members also wrote to Robert E. Lee, former commander of the Confederate army, and asked him to become their leader. But Lee, who was in poor health at that time, did not want to be associated with an illegal organization. He wrote back to say that, while he approved of the Klan's actions, his support must remain "invisible."

Inspired by Lee's words, the Klan members adopted "Invisible Empire" as the nickname for their group. They asked Forrest to become their "Grand Wizard," or leader. Hundreds of *Klaverns*—independent bands of Klansmen—formed in Tennessee, Alabama, and Georgia, and soon more than 100,000 men throughout the United States were members of the secret organization.

During the late 1860s, the Klan threatened white people who sympathized with blacks or cooperated with northerners. They attacked blacks for not showing respect for whites or for trying to vote in elections. They punished blacks by beating them or by hanging them from tree limbs. In disguise and under cover of night, the Klan members ignored the nation's existing legal system and made their own laws in defiance of police and politicians who opposed them. By 1868, the U.S. Congressional Committee on Lawlessness reported that 373 freed slaves had been killed by whites—including Klan members—since the end of the Civil War.

In 1870, southerners were able to vote out of office members of many of the state agencies set up by the federal government after the Civil War. Because the South could now govern itself, Forrest decided that the Klan had accomplished its mission. He officially disbanded the organization and resigned as its leader. In 1871, Congress passed the Ku Klux Klan Act, which outlawed secret organizations that tried to deprive groups of people of their right to vote.

For a time, the Ku Klux Klan activities decreased, and the Southern economy recovered. Nevertheless, white southerners felt that black equality would cheat them out of their own rights and keep them poor. At the same time, many northerners were feeling resentments of their own. Waves of immigrants—many of them Roman Catholics or Jews—were arriving from Europe. These immigrants took jobs in northern factories and settled in poor urban ghettoes. Some northerners saw these immigrants, as well as the blacks who were arriving from the South, as a threat to their livelihood and to their way of life.

A tide of racial prejudice swept across the United States during World War I. This hostility worsened after the 1915 release of *Birth of a Nation*, which drew huge crowds in movie theaters. The film depicted the Klan's violent activities as heroic. According to the film, blacks had been content as slaves and freed blacks were a threat to the democratic system and to the future of the United States.

In Georgia, a man named William J. Simmons saw the success of the film as an opportunity to revive the Ku Klux Klan. In November 1915, Simmons led a small group of followers up the slopes of Stone Mountain near Atlanta, Georgia, where they took an oath to uphold the ancient traditions of the Klan. Since the night air was cold, they also lit a large wooden cross to provide heat and light for the ceremony. Klan members would later adopt the burning cross as one of their most potent symbols.

Simmons was born in Alabama in 1880. He fought in the Spanish-American War of 1898 and later began using the title of "colonel," although he never actually

Although the cross symbolizes peace and forgiveness for many people, Klan members use burning crosses to show their anger.

reached that rank. In the early years of the twentieth century, he became a Methodist minister. But in 1912, the Methodist Church suspended him for "moral impairment," saying he was too lazy and incompetent to work as a minister.

Simmons worked for a short time as a traveling salesman. Then he became an organizer for fraternal organizations and private clubs, such as the Freemasons and the Knights of Templar, which had special codes and rituals. Simmons rounded up members, receiving a percentage of the money they paid in dues. His talent as a recruiter and fund-raiser soon made him a wealthy man.

In 1912, Simmons was injured in a car accident and confined to bed for several months. During his recovery, he read about Nathan Bedford Forrest and the Ku Klux Klan activities of the nineteenth century. Learning about Forrest would inspire Simmons to revive the Klan as a national organization of patriotic white Protestants.

Simmons began to plan for a new Ku Klux Klan, one that would go beyond the anger and humiliation of the post–Civil War South. His Klan would use the fear and resentment that many white Americans were feeling toward blacks, immigrants, and Roman Catholics. Its members would defend what they saw as traditional American values: patriotism, capitalism, and Christian morality. The Klan would fight the country's moral decay and restore its own version of law and order. Although the original Klan accepted almost anyone who was white, the new Klan would be made up almost exclusively of Protestants who had been born in the United States.

To appeal to potential members, Simmons devised an elaborate organizational plan for the Klan, with powerful titles for Klan members. As the national leader, he would be the "Imperial Wizard" of the Klan. "Grand Dragons" would lead the eight national districts, and each local Klavern would be headed by an "Exalted Cyclops." (The cyclops was a one-eyed giant in ancient Greek mythology.) New members would pay a $10 initiation fee and take a vow to uphold and defend the principles of the Klan. The entire membership would meet in regular national conventions known as Klonvokations.

Nevertheless, the modern Klan was attracting few new members. In 1920, Simmons hired two skilled publicity agents, Edward Clarke and Elizabeth Tyler, to organize a national membership drive for the organization. In return for their work, Clarke and Tyler would receive 80 percent of the membership fees collected from every new member they brought in.

One year later, the Ku Klux Klan had more than 100,000 new members, making it about the same size the original Klan had been. To profit further from the organization, Simmons set up companies to manufacture sheets, hoods, and Ku Klux Klan symbols for his followers to wear. He also established companies to publish books about the Klan and real-estate offices to buy and sell property in the Klan's name.

As the Klaverns grew, their members fanned out across the countryside, carrying out the Klan mission. They whipped blacks and whites who crossed them. They beat men who left their wives and women who were unfaithful to their husbands. They attacked labor leaders who organized workers and lawyers who represented people accused of crimes.

In several states, especially in the South, the Klan became a powerful presence in courtrooms, police forces, and government. Sheriffs, attorneys, and police officers joined the organization. Klansmen were elected as mayors, judges, and legislators. Together the Klan made up a powerful underground network that controlled towns, cities, and entire counties.

But the rapid rise of the Klan also brought criticism. In September 1921, the New York *World* published a series of articles exposing the illegal and violent activities of the Klan. Confidential sources within the Klan had turned over membership lists and other information to the paper. The news stories accused the Klan of blackmail, financial swindling, conspiracy to break the law, and kidnapping. The *World* later received a Pulitzer Prize for its Klan exposé.

Articles in the *World* drew national attention, but they had little effect on Klan membership. In the early 1920s, many white Protestants in both northern and southern states strongly supported the Klan's mission. They were fearful of the growing number of blacks in the United States, and they did not think Roman Catholics should be elected to any political office. They viewed immigrants and Jewish people as threats to the nation and thought the United States was in a dangerous state of moral decline. In their eyes, the Prohibition era of the 1920s had brought gangsters, corruption, lawlessness, a rising rate of divorce, and a general lack of respect for old-fashioned virtues.

After the New York *World* articles appeared, the U.S. Congress held hearings on the Klan and called on Colonel Simmons to testify. On the witness stand, Simmons defended his organization and denied any knowledge of Klan violence. He promised to dismiss Klan members who violated the law. Simmons's answers and his confident performance before Congress convinced many of its members that he had the Klan under control.

In reality, the Klan was spinning out of Simmons's control. Many members believed that he, Clarke, and Tyler were simply using the organization as a scheme to get rich. Hiram Wesley Evans, a Klansman from Dallas, and David Stephenson, a Klan leader in Indiana, saw the turmoil as a chance to remove Simmons from the organization and to take over the Klan.

In the autumn of 1922, Stephenson and Evans developed a plan. Shortly before an important Klonvokation took place on Thanksgiving Day in Atlanta, Stephenson convinced the Imperial Wizard that other members of the Klan were about to vote him out of office. If Simmons would allow Hiram Evans to become the new Imperial Wizard temporarily, then the two men would work to reward Simmons with an even grander title—"Emperor." Simmons agreed.

WHEN the lion eats grass like an ox
   And the grub-worm swallows the whale,
When the terrapin knits woolen socks
   And the hare is out-run by the snail,
When the tail of the 'possum grows hair
   And butterflies dwell in the sea,
When the raccoon's tail becomes bare
   And man enjoys the company of the flea,
When serpents walk upright like men
   And doodle-bugs travel like frogs,
When grasshoppers shall feed on the hen
   And feathers are found on hogs,
When the monkey ceases to swing by his tail
   And the baboon crawls on his back,
When the waters of the ocean shall fail
   And Gibraltar is carried in a sack,
When Thomas-cats swim in the air
   And elephants roost on trees,
When insects in summer are rare
   And snuff never makes people sneeze,
When the American eagle shall change
   And become a wabbling canary in a cage,
When dogs no longer have mange
   And old maids are not ashamed of their age,
When fish creep over dry land
   And mules on bicycles ride,
When foxes lay eggs in the sand
   And women in dress takes no pride,
When the devil has become a real saint
   And cynics no longer shall scorn,
When society women no longer use paint
   And boy babies cease to be born,
When the flowers shall die from the earth
   And the stars shall cease to shine,
When grave yards become theatres of mirth
   And the Hebrew shall feast upon swine,
When the darky no longer sees ghosts
   And his hair is minus the kink,
When the hobo refuses beef roasts
   And the human mind ceases to think,

When the pickaninny refuses watermelon
   And the North Pole is a banana patch,
When a murderer is no longer a felon
   And chick for worms will not scratch,
When the mole ceases to burrow into the ground
   And cat-fish grow fur like minks,
When a sphere is other than round
   And gophers play golf at the links,
When the Dutchman no longer drinks beer
   And girls get to preaching on time,
When the billy-goat butts from the rear
   And treason is no longer a crime,
When the humming-bird brays like an ass
   And limberger smells like cologne,
When plow points are made out of glass
   And the hearts of real Americans are stone,
When gold loses its value as cash
   And whiskey no longer makes drunk,
When diamonds are discarded as trash
   And radium is regarded as junk,
When fire no longer will burn
   And water ceases to make wet,
When courting couples all taffy shall spurn
   And the sun refuses to set,
When the clouds no longer give rain
   And toads have wings like bats,
When colic no longer gives pain
   And hoofs are found on rats,
When dollars shall drop from the sky
   And no crime a man's mother-in-law to kill,
When it is no longer a sin to lie
   And the tongue of the tattler is still,
When the Irishman loses his native wit
   And gone his appetite for ale,
When giraffs in rocking chairs shall sit
   And the June-bug whistles like a quail,
When peanuts grow on a Chinaman's head
   And wool on a hydraulic ram,
Then the Ku Klux Klan will be dead
   And the country won't be worth a double d—— (dim

FINIS

William Simmons wrote this poem, "When the Ku Klux Klan Will Be Dead," to express his belief that the Klan was indestructible.

72

After the convention, Evans ran the Ku Klux Klan as the new Imperial Wizard, while Stephenson became a Grand Dragon with control of the Klan in 22 states. Simmons, meanwhile, found that the title of Emperor gave him no real power or authority in the Klan. The following year, Elizabeth Tyler quit, and Edward Clarke was convicted of violating the Mann Act, a federal law that prohibited transporting women across state lines for immoral purposes.

Under Evans's leadership, the wave of Klan violence continued in the mid-1920s. By 1924, the national Klan claimed more than 2 million members. Stephenson resigned from the national Klan and formed his own Indiana Klan. That year, the Klan-supported candidates in Indiana won the governor's race as well as control of the state legislature.

At the same time, the Klan was dividing into feuding factions. Evans's supporters in the Indiana legislature blocked laws proposed by Stephenson's allies. A scandal developed in 1925 when Stephenson was convicted of murdering a woman he had been dating. After Stephenson went to prison, the Indiana Klan gradually declined.

Evans's success in ousting Simmons planted the seeds of a breakup that occurred in the 1930s. Allies and opponents of Hiram Evans openly feuded over the organization's finances and policies. Stories of beatings, blackmail, and murder spread as Klan leaders sued each other in public courtrooms. As the Great Depression wore on

Although many people do not believe that the Ku Klux Klan and other racist organizations should be allowed to hold public demonstrations, the U.S. Supreme Court has ruled that—like any other group—they can hold public rallies so long as they do not break any laws in the process.

and millions of Americans suffered unemployment and worsening poverty, Klan membership began to fall. Simmons, meanwhile, retired to his home in Alabama, where he died in 1946.

The Klan, however, remained active in criticizing Franklin D. Roosevelt, who was elected president in 1932. President Roosevelt spearheaded several new policies to help the nation recover from the Depression. But Klan leaders saw the New Deal as a Communist plot to destroy the United States. The Klan also allied itself with the *Bund*, an organization of German-Americans that openly supported German dictator Adolf Hitler.

During World War II, the U.S. Department of the Treasury sued the Klan for back taxes owed on membership dues. The bill came to $685,000. Unable to pay the fine, the national organization collapsed, leaving the Ku Klux Klan in the hands of local leaders scattered across the South and the Midwest. Only a few local branches of the Klan survived.

After World War II ended in 1945, the Klan remained relatively quiet for several years. But the civil rights movement of the 1960s in the South revived the organization. In 1954, the U.S. Supreme Court ordered the desegregation of public schools. Southern schools that had only educated white students had to begin admitting blacks as well. Soon afterward, white northerners were arriving in southern states to help register blacks to vote. Many southerners saw desegregation as another attack by the North on the South. To fight back, they created new versions of the old Ku Klux Klan.

In 1961, Robert Shelton founded the United Klans of America in Georgia. Shelton, who adopted the title of Imperial Wizard, headed one of the most violent and dangerous racist groups in the country. He hated all blacks and Jews, along with any product that had been

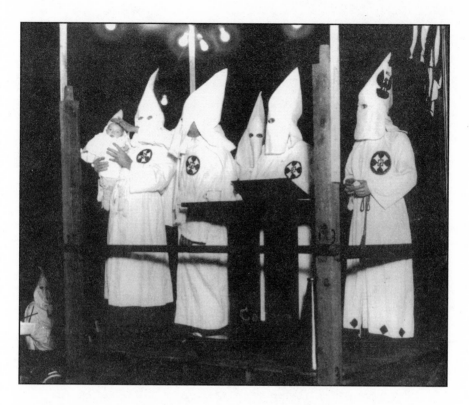

Hooded and robed Klansmen address their followers, calling attention to one of the group's newest members.

manufactured outside of the United States. He suspected that the government's decision to add fluoride to tap water was part of a conspiracy to take over the United States through mind control.

The Klan under Shelton carried out several murders in Georgia and Alabama. As the federal government sent in troops to force southern schools to desegregate, Shelton's followers responded by bombing a church in

Birmingham, Alabama. Four African-American girls were killed in the explosion. During the 1960s, other southern Klan members were convicted of murdering peaceful civil rights activists.

In 1980, six Klan members were arrested for killing four anti-Klan activists in Greensboro, North Carolina, but they were found not guilty by an all-white jury. The following year, two Klansmen took the law into their own hands in Birmingham. After a jury returned a verdict of not guilty for a black man accused of murdering a white police officer, the Klansmen went looking for revenge. They kidnapped a different black man, named Michael Donald, from a street corner, beat him, slashed his throat, and then hung his corpse from a tree.

By this time, however, anti-Klan forces in the South were better organized than they had been in the past. An Atlanta lawyer named Morris Dees convinced Michael Donald's mother, Beulah May Donald, to sue Shelton and the United Klans for damages. The two murderers, who had been arrested and convicted in 1983, testified that Shelton's group had encouraged them to carry out the crime. The court found the United Klans liable for $7 million in damages. The case bankrupted Shelton and his organization.

Nevertheless, other Klan groups survived. Former Klan member David Duke became a representative in the Louisiana legislature in 1989. Many people considered Duke, who was articulate and well groomed,

*David Duke, a Louisiana state legislator, made strong
runs for both the U.S. Senate (1990) and governor
(1991), despite his past affiliation with the Ku Klux
Klan.*

to be a respectable symbol of opposition to welfare,
busing students to school to achieve desegregation, and
affirmative-action programs, which encouraged the hiring of minorities. Duke even made a run for president in
1980, 1984, 1988, and 1992. During this period, the
Klan continued to receive negative attention, and some
Klan members were arrested for attacking blacks.

Duke's campaigns for high office failed, but Klan
activities have continued. Some Klan members have

continued with the old mission of denying civil rights to blacks. Others have changed the Klan's message. Many contemporary Klan members now say that their group fights only for whites, not against blacks.

The Ku Klux Klan has also helped to inspire other racist organizations, such as the neo-Nazi group White Aryan Resistance. No longer fighting for the glory and traditions of the South, the Klan and similar groups of the 1990s survive as purely racist organizations that thrive on fear, resentment, and ignorance.

A group of teenagers displays the Nazi swastika to show that they do not want racial minorities in their community.

Catholic priest Charles Coughlin (1891-1979) won many supporters—and many enemies—through his angry radio broadcasts during the 1930s.

5

Father Charles Coughlin
The Radio Priest

*D*uring the Great Depression of the 1930s, millions of people across the globe grew fearful as they lost their jobs and struggled to provide food for their families. The resentment that many people felt became a useful tool for powerful demagogues, who tried to intensify and manipulate this widespread fear and paranoia. In Germany and Italy, militant nationalists—called *fascists*—blamed Jews and Communists for the hard times.

The democratic system in the United States prevented the nation from falling under control of dictators such as Adolf Hitler of Germany or Benito Mussolini of Italy. But feelings of anger and suspicion were spreading across the nation nonetheless.

Many people thought some conspiracy must have caused the vast and wealthy United States to suffer such an economic catastrophe. The nation was ready for a skilled demagogue to put all of this widespread fear and anger to work. Such a man did arrive, and his name was Father Charles Coughlin.

Benito Mussolini (1883-1945), who turned Italy into a dictatorship during the 1920s, tolerated no dissent from his iron-fisted authority, and eventually led his people into a disastrous war.

Charles Edward Coughlin was born into an Irish-Catholic family in Ontario, Canada, on October 25, 1891. His parents sent him to the parish school of St. Mary's and then to high school and college in the city of Toronto. Coughlin worked hard in school and was a talented speaker. He knew that his family and his teachers expected great things from him, and he always strived to meet their expectations.

Although Coughlin wanted to be a politician, his parents pressured him into becoming a Catholic priest. Charles obeyed their wishes. In 1914, he entered St. Basil's, a Catholic college in Waco, Texas. Two years later, he was ordained as a priest. Afterward, the Roman Catholic Church assigned Coughlin to teach at Assumption College in the town of Sandwich, Ontario, near the border with Michigan. At Assumption, he taught English, logic, and psychology. On Sundays, he crossed the border to preach in Catholic churches in Detroit.

Coughlin's talent and energy soon won him notice from his superiors in the Church. In 1923, they assigned him to St. Leo's Church in Detroit. Three years later, Coughlin's friend, Bishop Michael Gallagher, asked him to become the priest of a new church in the Detroit suburb of Royal Oak. The church was called the Shrine of the Little Flower. Gallagher had founded the church to honor Saint Thérèse, a Catholic saint whose nickname was the "little flower of Jesus."

Father Coughlin, who had wanted to become a politician instead of a priest, often spoke about the government and foreign events in his sermons.

The new assignment was a tough challenge for Coughlin. Royal Oak was a stronghold of the Ku Klux Klan, a fanatical enemy of the Catholic Church. To welcome Father Coughlin and the Catholics to Royal Oak, the Klan burned a cross on the lawn of the new church. The burning cross was a symbol that members of the Ku Klux Klan had traditionally used to frighten their enemies.

Neither discouraged nor frightened by the Klan, Coughlin brought hundreds of new members into the small congregation. He never lacked for ideas. To attract worshippers, he arranged for several baseball players from the Detroit Tigers to attend his church service one

Sunday. Another Sunday, Babe Ruth and several of his famous New York Yankee teammates stood at the doorways holding collection boxes. They helped Coughlin to collect $10,000 in donations that morning.

After Babe Ruth's appearance, Sunday attendance at the Shrine of the Little Flower grew steadily. But Father Coughlin was never entirely satisfied with his accomplishments. He wanted to lead a bigger congregation, to reach a wider audience. In 1926, Coughlin asked Leo Fitzpatrick, the manager of radio station WJR in Detroit, if he could start broadcasting his Sunday sermons over WJR. Fitzpatrick liked the idea, but he asked the priest to pay the station $58 each week to cover the cost of the broadcasts. Coughlin agreed.

Father Coughlin, pictured here with young members of his congregation, believed that his radio broadcasts would help to protect the future of the United States.

Father Coughlin made his first radio broadcast on October 17, 1926. He knew that many of his listeners were not Catholics, perhaps not even Christians. So instead of giving a biblical sermon, he talked about the general importance of religion. After the first broadcast, five listeners wrote the priest to express their appreciation, and many more people wrote to WJR to compliment the show. Fitzpatrick decided to allow the new feature to continue.

Sunday after Sunday, Father Coughlin's sermons drew a growing audience of regular listeners. Detroit newspaper columnists gave the priest favorable reviews, and the Shrine of the Little Flower enjoyed higher attendance and larger donations. By the autumn of 1927, Coughlin was broadcasting his sermons to several midwestern states. Hundreds of listeners were moving into Royal Oak to be near "the radio priest," as Coughlin was sometimes called.

With the rising tide of money that was flowing into the Shrine's treasury, Coughlin made plans to build an even larger Shrine of the Little Flower. The new shrine, completed in October 1933, was an octagonal (eight-sided) church that cost $1 million to construct and could seat up to 2,600 people. A 180-foot tower connected to the church held a small broadcasting studio and offices for the growing staff.

By 1930, the Great Depression had taken hold of the United States. Coughlin, who had always held strong opinions about the government and the economy, began to discuss business, culture, politics, and foreign affairs on the radio. He knew people were looking for an explanation of the hard times they were going through. They were also looking for someone to blame for the Great Depression. Coughlin faulted socialists, international bankers, wealthy businessmen, and the failure of the U. S. government to do anything about the economic crisis. He also used his broadcast to attack writers and politicians whom he personally disliked.

During the Great Depression, many people waited for hours in bread lines to receive food from government programs or charitable organizations.

Coughlin had several suggestions for ending the Great Depression. He wanted the U.S. Department of the Treasury to print more money and distribute it to those who needed it most. Coughlin also suggested that the rich sell their gold and silver and then invest their money. With increased investment, Coughlin believed the economy would improve.

In the autumn of 1930, Father Coughlin signed a contract to broadcast over the national CBS radio network. Soon, 40 million listeners in 23 states were tuning in every Sunday to listen to his opinions about the Depression. Coughlin's straightforward manner convinced many listeners that he was an expert in economics and political affairs. Many people simply enjoyed hearing his voice, which they found mellow and heartwarming.

Father Coughlin also asked people to send contributions to his church to support the broadcasts. Thousands of envelopes with small donations arrived at the Shrine of the Little Flower every week. Coughlin had to hire 106 clerks and 4 personal secretaries just to handle the stacks of letters, checks, and cash that were piling up in his office, as well as the numerous requests for copies of his radio speeches.

But Coughlin's opinions soon got him into trouble with the network. When CBS officials asked him to tone down his attacks on banks and big businesses, Coughlin responded by spending his entire broadcast on January 4, 1931, accusing the network of trying to censor him. CBS retaliated by refusing to renew Coughlin's contract. Despite this setback, Coughlin forged ahead and immediately organized an independent network of stations to carry his show. By 1932, he had 27 stations signed, and by the mid-1930s, he was broadcasting coast to coast.

This growing base of support convinced Coughlin that he should involve himself in national politics. During the 1932 presidential campaign, he publicly threw his support to Democratic candidate Franklin D. Roosevelt. Coughlin became a strong supporter of the social programs—known collectively as the New Deal—that Roosevelt intended to use to combat the Depression. Coughlin also sought an important position in the Roosevelt administration. Roosevelt met with Coughlin while campaigning for president. Although he was careful not to anger the popular priest, Roosevelt considered Coughlin's views to be extremely radical and decided to keep his distance from him.

Roosevelt won the election, and his New Deal programs were well underway by 1934. But Coughlin was soon at odds with the president. He used his broadcasts to attack Roosevelt's administration, which he said was full of Communists who favored a society where the government owned all businesses and everyone earned an equal wage.

As the Great Depression continued, the priest also accused Roosevelt of not doing enough to help the underprivileged. Then, Coughlin began to say that

Though a popular president, Franklin D. Roosevelt (1882-1945) was harshly criticized during Father Coughlin's radio broadcasts. Roosevelt, who held office from 1933 to 1945, initiated the New Deal to relieve Americans' misery during the Great Depression.

Roosevelt was part of an international conspiracy that was undermining the economy of the United States and forcing millions of workers into poverty. At the same time, Father Coughlin was also using his broadcasts to urge the government to free silver prices, which would allow the value of silver to rise. In April 1934, the U.S. Treasury Department discovered that Amy Collins, the treasurer of the Radio League of the Little Flower, Inc., had invested heavily in silver. If silver prices rose, Amy Collins and Coughlin's church would have made a fortune.

The scandal that unfolded made Coughlin appear greedy and corrupt, and he lost many loyal listeners. But the negative publicity did not deter him from politics. In December 1934, Coughlin created the National Union for Social Justice (NUSJ). He announced that this new organization would defend the right of private owner-ship and protect U.S. citizens from big business and the federal government.

Coughlin saw the presidential elections of 1936 as his chance to steer the nation and its leaders toward his views. He launched a nationwide speaking tour and said that if the government did not adopt or acknowledge his economic policies, he would run his own candidate against Roosevelt. Coughlin let loose a bitter attack in the pages of *Social Justice*, the NUSJ's weekly newspaper. He called Roosevelt a liar and accused the president of planning to set up a Communist dictatorship in the United States.

In a June 1936 broadcast, Coughlin announced that he was forming a new political party—the Union Party. He named William Lemke, a congressman from North Dakota, as his presidential candidate. Coughlin pledged to leave radio unless Lemke received 9 million votes in the upcoming election.

As a Roman Catholic priest, Coughlin could not run for office himself, and his involvement in national politics angered some of his superiors in the Catholic

Church. During the 1936 campaign, the church asked Coughlin to reduce his political activities and apologize to President Roosevelt. Although the priest did apologize, he continued his intense speaking schedule in support of Union Party candidate William Lemke.

Catholic officials at the Vatican in Rome, Italy, still worried about Coughlin. They did not want the church to appear to be taking sides in an election. The Vatican sent Eugenio Cardinal Pacelli (later elected Pope Pius XII) to handle the situation. Pacelli insisted that Bishop Gallagher make Father Coughlin return to his religious duties. Pacelli told the bishop to order Coughlin out of politics after the 1936 election. Gallagher reluctantly agreed to do what was asked of him.

On election day 1936, President Roosevelt won by a landslide, carrying 46 states and losing in only Maine and Vermont. William Lemke, on the other hand, had proved to be an uninspiring speaker and had attracted little public support. Out of 45 million votes cast, Lemke received just 900,000—only ten percent of the number that Coughlin had hoped for. Coughlin discovered the hard truth of all third-party campaigns: When voters finally go to the polls, they cast their votes for the candidates who have a chance of winning.

For a short time, Father Coughlin honored Bishop Gallagher's request that he leave politics. Coughlin also kept his own promise to end his radio career if Lemke did not receive 9 million votes in the election. But after the bishop died in January 1937, Coughlin went back on the air, claiming that Gallagher's last request had been that Coughlin resume his broadcasts.

The results of the 1936 election had convinced Coughlin that an international conspiracy was at hand. He announced that President Roosevelt, the Communists, and Jews were all working together to destroy the capitalist system and impose a worldwide dictatorship. He allowed no opposing views to be spoken on his show and ignored any evidence that would contradict his theories. Like many demagogues, Coughlin regarded those who disagreed with him as his enemies.

To organize his followers to fight this conspiracy, Coughlin founded the Christian Front, which urged people to buy only from Christian merchants. Members of the Christian Front attacked Jews on the streets and in the workplace. Street brawls between members of Coughlin's organization and his opponents broke out in several cities.

The same thing was happening in Europe, where German dictator Adolf Hitler was blaming the Jewish people for many of that nation's problems. Hitler's policies were forcing Jews out of their jobs, their homes, and out of the country.

In his radio broadcasts, Coughlin defended Hitler's actions as a necessary defense against Communism. The priest claimed that Jews had not spoken out against the way the Communists in the Soviet Union were treating Christians. So, Coughlin insisted, Christians in the

United States should not concern themselves with Hitler's treatment of the Jews in Germany.

Journalists harshly criticized Father Coughlin for his views, and several radio stations dropped his Sunday broadcasts. Other stations worried about the controversy surrounding the priest and his opinions. When WMCA, the radio station that broadcast Coughlin in New York City, asked him to submit scripts of his programs to the station in advance, the priest refused. WMCA then dropped the broadcast—an action that brought a crowd of angry pro-Coughlin demonstrators to the streets in front of the station.

In 1939, Hitler ordered his army to invade Poland, an act that touched off World War II. Although many U.S. citizens strongly opposed the Nazis, Coughlin supported Hitler as the best defense Europe and the United States had against Communism and the Soviet Union. Coughlin also saw Roosevelt's support of Great Britain in the war as another example of the international Jewish conspiracy. To support his views, Coughlin began printing Nazi propaganda pieces in *Social Justice*.

These pro-Nazi opinions stirred even more public outrage. A wave of protest against the show prompted the National Association of Broadcasters to establish new rules for radio broadcasts. Stations were now to set aside free air time for public-service announcements and programs that discussed controversial issues. Those who wished to discuss these issues, however, would have to submit their scripts in advance to the station for approval before they could be broadcast. As a result of this rule, individuals such as Father Coughlin could no longer simply buy air time and use it to express whatever views they wished.

This new policy prompted many radio stations to cancel their contracts with Father Coughlin. As his radio

Although many evangelists now speak to television viewers, Father Coughlin was one of the first religious leaders to reach the public over the airwaves.

audience shrank, donations to the Shrine of the Little Flower also fell. In the autumn of 1940, Coughlin announced his retirement from the air.

Coughlin's stand on World War II had appealed to many Americans who did not want to get involved in another bloody European conflict. But when Germany's ally, Japan, attacked the U.S. military base at Pearl Harbor in December 1941, the public mood in the United States changed immediately. Nearly all U.S. citizens supported Roosevelt's determination to enter and win the war.

With the United States officially at war, Coughlin found himself the target of a federal investigation. In 1942, the Federal Bureau of Investigation (FBI) raided Coughlin's offices in Royal Oak. For his fiery accusations against the Roosevelt administration, and for the Nazi propaganda that ran in *Social Justice*, the government accused Coughlin of *sedition*—inciting rebellion against the government.

The Roosevelt administration wanted to avoid a trial and any more clashes with the priest. Likewise, the Catholic Church sought to avoid further controversy over Coughlin. Federal officials asked Archbishop Edward Mooney of Detroit to stop Coughlin from further public speeches. If Coughlin cooperated, the government would drop its charge of sedition against him.

Unlike Bishop Gallagher, Archbishop Mooney did not support Father Coughlin. On May 1, 1942, Mooney ordered Coughlin to return to his church and cease all of his political activities. If Coughlin did not obey this order, the bishop promised to expel the priest from the Church.

Coughlin obeyed Mooney and turned his attention back to his loyal congregation in Royal Oak. *Social Justice* lost its mailing privileges and closed down, and the Christian Front disappeared. For the next 37 years, Coughlin would remain in Michigan and stay out of politics and national affairs. He tended to his duties as a priest until he was asked to retire in 1966. He spent his remaining years at his home in Birmingham, Michigan, and died on October 27, 1979.

*Wisconsin senator Joseph McCarthy (1908-1957)
spread fear across the United States by claiming the
federal government was filled with Communists.*

6

Joseph McCarthy
The Anti-Communist

*W*hile growing up during the early twentieth century, Joseph Raymond McCarthy was determined to make a name for himself. Born on November 14, 1908, young Joseph and his five brothers learned about hard work and discipline while working on their father's dairy farm just outside of Appleton, Wisconsin. Joe dropped out of school in the eighth grade and started his own chicken-farming operation. At age 19, he became the manager of a local grocery store. His sharp wit and friendly manner made up for his lack of education. Everyone who knew him was sure he would go far.

When he was 20 years old, Joe McCarthy went back to school. After only a year of study, he passed four years' worth of courses and was awarded his high school diploma. In 1929, he enrolled at Marquette University in Milwaukee, Wisconsin, where he studied for the bar examination that would allow him to practice law. After graduating from college, he joined a law firm in the town of Waupaca.

Joe McCarthy had little interest in the difficult and often solitary work that takes up much of a lawyer's day. Instead of trying cases in court, he spent his time playing poker with his friends. He brought few new clients to the firm and soon began to feel restless and bored. Looking for some kind of change, he soon left Waupaca and joined a law firm in Shawano, Wisconsin.

In 1939, one of McCarthy's new law partners, Mike Eberlein, announced he was running for the post of circuit court judge. Convinced that politics was where his real talents lay, McCarthy decided to join the Republican Party and run for the same position. McCarthy threw himself into the election campaign with great zeal and confidence. Making speeches, traveling long distances, and shaking hands came naturally to McCarthy, and he won the election.

As a circuit judge, McCarthy traveled to courtrooms in several towns and made rulings on hundreds of cases. Many lawyers began to notice that McCarthy seemed more interested in finishing up as many legal cases as possible than in carefully reviewing evidence or listening to witnesses. McCarthy's energy impressed some of his colleagues, but others saw him as an overly ambitious man who had his sights set on a higher goal. The Wisconsin Supreme Court, in fact, criticized McCarthy for his "abuse of judicial power" during one case involving economic issues.

When the United States entered World War II—joining several European nations in the fight against Germany, Italy, and Japan—McCarthy enlisted in the U.S. Marines and was assigned to the Pacific theater as an intelligence officer. McCarthy's job was to gather information from pilots returning from combat and bombing missions. He sometimes accompanied the pilots on their missions over the Pacific, but he never flew a plane and rarely held a weapon. Nevertheless, McCarthy told reporters in Wisconsin that he had been a "fighting pilot." Many of his friends and acquaintances believed his colorful war stories and were proud to know a real war hero.

After World War II ended in 1945, McCarthy ran for the U.S. Senate seat held by Republican Robert M. La Follette Jr. The senator came from one of the most renowned political families in Wisconsin. However, many conservative Republicans thought La Follette was too liberal. McCarthy decided to take advantage of this situation by accusing La Follette of being a Communist.

McCarthy was willing to do almost anything to win a Senate seat, and his tactics worked. Many people who had supported La Follette in the past, especially strongly anti-Communist urban workers, believed McCarthy and shifted their allegiance to him. McCarthy beat La Follette in the Senate primary, and went on to defeat Democratic candidate Howard J. McMurray, whom he also accused of being "communistically inclined."

At first, McCarthy did poorly in the U.S. Senate. He wrote no major legislation of his own. Even worse, he faced accusations of accepting money from lobbyists in return for political favors. After becoming friendly with real-estate developers, McCarthy fought against public-housing projects that would have hurt the developers. Similarly, his attempt to lift controls on the price of sugar was intended to benefit his supporters from Pepsi-Cola and the Allied Molasses Company. Unhappy with his questionable actions, many of his colleagues began calling McCarthy the "Pepsi-Cola Kid."

McCarthy also gained bad publicity for interfering in a congressional investigation of a massacre in Malmédy, Belgium, that had occurred during World War II. The United States had evidence that German officers in Malmédy had ordered the killing of 150 captured U.S. soldiers and 100 Belgian civilians. Forty-three Germans had been found guilty of the crime and sentenced to die. Nevertheless, McCarthy said that the U.S. had used torture to get confessions out of the Germans. His motive was to please German-American voters and supporters in his home state of Wisconsin. But

Communist opponents of the United States in Germany and throughout the rest of Europe used McCarthy's false accusations in their propaganda against the United States.

McCarthy was still looking for an issue that would make him a national hero. He soon found it in the growing fear of Communism and the threat of the Soviet Union. After the end of World War II, the United States and the Soviet Union became the two major political powers in the world. The worldwide growth of the Communist movement, which worked to overthrow capitalist economic systems, raised overwhelming suspicion in many Americans. This fear prompted the "Cold War," a massive buildup of nuclear weapons and military forces in both the Soviet Union and the United States.

The Communist scare during the 1950s prompted many U.S. citizens to take action against suspected Communist sympathizers. Several states formed

During the Cold War, the United States and the Soviet Union each built massive numbers of nuclear weapons to deter the other from starting a war.

committees to investigate "un-American activities." Many businesses and universities demanded that their employees take oaths of loyalty to the United States. Likewise, companies often conducted thorough background checks on their employees' personal lives.

The Federal Bureau of Investigation (FBI) began arresting several government employees who were suspected of spying for the Soviet Union. In 1950, Julius Rosenberg and his wife, Ethel, were arrested for allegedly sending classified military information about nuclear weapons to the Soviet Union. (This cloud of suspicion was reminiscent of the "Palmer Raids" of 1920, when

Julius Rosenberg (1918-1953), an electrical engineer for the U.S. government, and his wife, Ethel (1916-1953), were found guilty of sending classified information about nuclear weapons to the Soviet Union. Many Americans were upset when the Rosenbergs were executed on June 19, 1953, because they felt the death penalty was too severe for their crime.

U.S. attorney general A. Mitchell Palmer had 4,000 anarchists, socialists, and communists arrested for being a "menace" to the nation. Likewise, many entertainers suspected of being Communists had lost their jobs and been "blacklisted" from Hollywood during the 1940s.)

With another senatorial election coming up in 1952, Joe McCarthy again used the public's anti-Communist feelings to help him hold on to his Senate seat. In a speech given to the Republican Club of Wheeling, West Virginia, McCarthy announced, "I have here in my hand a list of 205 names known to the secretary of state as being members of the Communist Party who nevertheless are still working and shaping the policy of the State Department." (He later admitted the paper he waved in the air was merely his laundry list.)

As planned, McCarthy's spectacular accusation gained national news coverage. Officials in the U.S. Department of State angrily denied his accusations, but McCarthy's fellow Republicans came out in support of him. Democratic presidents had occupied the White House for the previous 20 years, and many Republicans hoped this scandal might help their candidate win the next presidential election.

McCarthy followed up his Wheeling speech with more accusations. In the Senate, he announced that President Harry Truman's administration was allowing a vast network of Communist spies to operate within the government. When pressed for evidence to back up his accusations, McCarthy produced a list of names, which he held aloft at every opportunity.

In fact, the senator was using a list of people the State Department had either already investigated and cleared of being Communists or who had already resigned from the department for one reason or another. McCarthy, however, never mentioned this fact.

Although federal officials knew there were probably only a few Communists working for the government—since those who had been discovered had been fired—few people had the courage to express their doubts openly. By this time, Joseph McCarthy was well known for his ability to cast suspicions on anyone who opposed him. People knew they could easily lose their jobs and permanently damage their careers if they even appeared to be sympathetic to the Soviet Union or to the Communist system.

To investigate McCarthy's claims, the U.S. Senate formed a committee under the direction of Senator Millard E. Tydings of Maryland. At the witness table, McCarthy claimed to have top-secret FBI information on Soviet spies, but he never offered any proof to verify his charges. Nor would he charge anyone specifically with a crime. Instead, he claimed that the committee would have to produce evidence and charges on its own. Not everyone believed him. Senators Margaret Chase Smith of Maine and Estes Kefauver from Tennessee were two politicians willing to speak out against McCarthy.

After Senator Margaret Chase Smith (1897-1995) of Maine spoke out against the wave of anti-Communist hysteria, Joseph McCarthy dismissed Smith as "Snow White" and called her supporters "the seven dwarfs."

The Tydings Committee, which was sympathetic to McCarthy, did its best to assist the senator. Additionally, President Truman offered the committee access to restricted State Department files. McCarthy, however, ridiculed the offer and charged officials with deliberately altering the files to protect the Communist spies working within the department. When FBI director J. Edgar Hoover disputed McCarthy's claims, the senator charged that the government was covering up evidence.

Millard Tydings (1890-1961) already had a strong reputation as an attorney and United States senator before heading the committee to investigate Senator Joseph McCarthy's claims in 1950.

After four months of investigations, the Tydings Committee issued a scathing report on McCarthy and his charges. According to the report, the Wisconsin senator's accusations were completely false. Nevertheless, public support for McCarthy was growing across the United States. The powerful chain of Hearst newspapers backed him up in its articles and editorials. Many people were sending McCarthy money to help him with investigations. The entire nation was gripped by suspicion and fear, and millions of people were convinced that McCarthy was telling the truth.

After the Senate committee issued its report, McCarthy vowed to get his revenge on Senator Tydings. During the senatorial election in Maryland, McCarthy supported John Marshall Butler, a Baltimore lawyer who was running against Tydings for a Senate seat. McCarthy's office used campaign literature to hurt Tydings's reputation. Additionally, the *Washington Times-Herald*—a Hearst newspaper that had printed the literature—altered a photo to show Tydings posing with Earl Browder, a Communist leader in the United States. Tydings lost the election.

McCarthy, who had been reelected in 1952, had a loyal staff, a secret network of supporters in the government, and his own congressional committee. After the United States entered the Korean War, in which the United States was helping South Korea oppose the Communist government of North Korea, McCarthy had yet another opportunity to use anti-Communist hysteria to his advantage.

The Wisconsin senator charged that George C. Marshall, the U.S. secretary of defense, was deliberately trying to lose the war. Although Marshall was a World War II hero and commanded widespread respect in the United States, McCarthy knew his charges of disloyalty would generate a great deal of publicity. Marshall retired several months after McCarthy's attack, but he did receive belated recognition when he was awarded the Nobel Peace Prize in 1953.

McCarthy also investigated the United States Information Agency (USIA), which runs U.S. libraries located in foreign cities. Many government agencies cooperated with McCarthy solely out of fear. In April 1953, McCarthy sent two of his assistants, Roy Cohn and David Schine, to several European cities to track down Communist influence in the USIA libraries. (Before working with McCarthy, Schine had published his own anti-Communist pamphlets and put them in the rooms of hotels owned by his wealthy family.) Schine and Cohn browsed through the libraries and found many books that they said promoted Communism, including works by Russian and American writers who were sympathetic to Communist ideas. The U.S. State Department then banned these books, forcing libraries to remove them from their shelves.

In the summer of 1953, the U.S. Army drafted David Schine after he and Cohn returned from his trip to Europe. Anxious to help Schine avoid entering the army as an enlisted man, Cohn and McCarthy badgered army officials to commission their colleague as an officer. When the army refused, McCarthy began a new campaign against the U.S. military, claiming that Robert Stevens, the secretary of the army, was holding Schine as a hostage to prevent investigations into the military by McCarthy's staff. The army then accused McCarthy of blackmail and interference.

The Senate ordered an investigation of the affair, and the Army-McCarthy hearings began on April 22, 1954. These were the first government hearings ever to be televised, and they drew much public attention. Many people saw the hearings as McCarthy's big chance to expose Communist infiltration in the government. Others hoped the hearings would finally enable the government to embarrass the Wisconsin senator and close down his committee.

McCarthy opened the hearings by badgering Stevens with questions and accusations for 14 consecutive days. The two men fought over major and minor details

Joseph McCarthy showed members of the Senate the areas of the United States where he believed Communists were active.

Joe McCarthy often claimed he had written proof to support his false accusations, even if the documents he had actually showed no evidence of disloyalty or Communist beliefs.

of Stevens's military career while McCarthy tried to depict Stevens as a Communist sympathizer. The senator also tried to show that Stevens knew Schine—a fact that Stevens denied.

During these 14 days, Joseph Welch, the army's lawyer, attacked McCarthy's own credibility. He tried to show that McCarthy was operating outside of his official duties to undermine the government. Welch also revealed that a confidential letter written by FBI director J. Edgar Hoover had secretly been given to the senator from an FBI operative who supported McCarthy. Under oath, McCarthy refused to give the name of his source. To the 2,000 people attending the hearing and the 20 million Americans watching the proceedings on television, McCarthy seemed to regard himself as being above the law and more important than everyone else in the Senate.

Welch then presented a photograph showing David Schine posing with Stevens. McCarthy had already used the photo to prove that Stevens had lied. But Welch showed that the photo was a fake—a composite that had been created in the darkroom.

McCarthy then turned on Welch, accusing him of recommending that attorney Frederick G. Fisher prepare for the hearings. McCarthy said that Fisher had once belonged to the Lawyers' Guild—an organization that had represented pro-Communist organizations. McCarthy implied that Welch himself was sympathetic to the Lawyers' Guild and to its clients.

Welch responded by describing a conversation he said he had had with Fred Fisher. Before the hearings, he had asked the young man if anything in his background was suspicious. Fisher had admitted belonging to the Lawyers' Guild. Wanting to avoid controversy, Welch then asked Fisher not to participate and to return to Boston. In front of a Senate hearing room and millions of television viewers, Welch blasted McCarthy for his devious and dishonest methods.

But McCarthy wasn't finished. Without evidence, he continued to insist that Welch had recommended Fisher. Simply by making the accusation, he was trying to cast suspicion on the army's lawyer. But he was making a grave mistake. Senator Karl Mundt, the chairman of the hearings, reported that, in fact, Welch had not recommended Fisher. Mundt's testimony exposed McCarthy as a liar.

With Mundt's statement backing him up, Welch drove home the point. Gazing angrily at McCarthy, he asked the senator, "Have you left no sense of decency?" The people seated in the hearing room burst into applause. McCarthy, unable to respond, slumped in his chair. Welch and Mundt had beaten McCarthy and humiliated him on television in full view of the U.S. public. The hearings soon came to an end.

Having seen Joe McCarthy up close, the nation quickly turned against him. In a Gallup opinion poll taken in January 1954, 50 percent of the respondents said they approved of McCarthy, and 29 percent said they were opposed to him. By that August, McCarthy's approval rating had dropped to 36 percent, with 51 percent of the public now opposing his ideas and actions. A wave of condemnation appeared in the press as well as in the Senate, where McCarthy had once intimidated the nation's most powerful legislators. On December 2, 1954, the Senate voted 67 to 22 formally to condemn McCarthy for his actions.

The Senate vote effectively ended McCarthy's career. The Republican Party abandoned him, and his support from the public disappeared. No longer in the public eye, McCarthy slid into depression and alcoholism. On May 2, 1957, he died of cirrhosis of the liver.

McCarthy's pursuit of Communists in the government gave new life to the term *witch-hunt*. Like the Puritan leaders of colonial Massachusetts, McCarthy had used the public's fear to cast suspicion on those who opposed him or whom he simply disliked. The Cold War hostilities between the United States and the Soviet Union had made this witch-hunt possible, but public exposure of McCarthy's tactics had brought it to a sudden end. By this time, *McCarthyism* had become a new term for the old practice of demagoguery.

George Lincoln Rockwell (1918-1967), leader of the American Nazi Party, believed that the nation should—at all costs—stop racial minorities from obtaining equal rights with whites.

116

7

George Lincoln Rockwell
An American Nazi

*I*n the early 1960s, a powerful movement spread across the South to end racial discrimination. Leaders of this civil rights movement rallied to give blacks the same opportunities as whites to vote, attend college, and hold down a job. Martin Luther King Jr. and other activists frequently used nonviolent marches, sit-ins, and rallies to campaign for these goals.

Many of the people who supported the movement were young college students from the North, who traveled throughout the South to participate in civil rights activities. But another group roaming the countryside at this time was not working for civil rights. Instead, they were fighting the civil rights movement with threatening words and violence. They traveled from town to town in a bus which carried the words "We Hate Race Mixing" on its side.

The young men in the van dressed in khaki shirts and black boots. They each wore an armband showing a *swastika*, the symbol used by the Nazi Party of Germany during World War II. They spoke in loud, angry voices, criticizing Jews, blacks, and Communists. A U.S. Navy veteran from Illinois named George Lincoln Rockwell was leading them. Not long after he had fought against Germany in World War II, Rockwell became one of the strongest Nazi supporters in the nation.

The Nazi movement in the United States started in the 1920s, long before Rockwell's involvement. After Adolf Hitler attempted to overthrow the German government in 1923, a group of Hitler's followers came to the United States to raise money for the German Nazis. In 1924, an organization called *Teutonia* was founded in Chicago. Sympathetic to the German Nazi Party, the group published a newspaper and formed similar groups—called *cells*—in a handful of other large cities.

By 1933, Teutonia still had only a few dozen members. In the same year, Adolf Hitler took power in Germany. He banned all opposition parties, jailed his opponents, and accused Jews and Communists of trying

George Lincoln Rockwell (right) and his followers traveled from city to city in a bus marked "hate."

to destroy Germany. Hitler also claimed that most Germans belonged to a race of people called "Aryans," who were descended from northern Europeans. According to Hitler, Aryans were superior to all other races and ethnic groups and were destined to rule the world. Hitler promised that Germany would soon build a powerful empire in Europe and establish Aryan supremacy.

Hitler's success spurred on his followers in the United States. The Swastika League, the Friends of Germany, and several other pro-Nazi groups formed in the United States. They recruited Americans of German ancestry, as well as German citizens living in the United States. With the help of Hitler's own propaganda department, they tried to improve relations between the U.S. government and Nazi Germany.

In March 1936, a German chemist named Fritz Julius Kuhn organized the German-American Bund in Buffalo, New York. He established strict rules for membership in the Bund. New recruits could not have any Jewish or African ancestry—they had to be pure Aryans. Members of the organization also had to support the ideals of Adolf Hitler and the Nazi Party.

Kuhn, who worked for the Ford Hospital laboratory in Detroit, tried to make his new group a replica of the German Nazi Party. He organized a paramilitary unit called the *Ordnungsdienst* (military service), whose members wore uniforms patterned after those worn by Nazi storm troopers—armed men who attacked Hitler's enemies in Germany.

Kuhn also organized the Youth Division, which prepared young people for full membership in the German-American Bund. At Youth Division summer camps in New York and New Jersey, and in smaller meeting places across the country, Bund leaders taught their followers Nazi songs and salutes. They explained the Nazi philosophy of German racial superiority and warned that Jews and non-Aryan immigrants posed a grave danger to the future of the United States. These Bund leaders believed that Germans should lead the way in turning the United States into a purely white nation.

The Bund enlisted thousands of new members across the country. Most large cities in the United States had a Bund group, whose members paid regular monthly dues of 75 cents. To many people in the United States, the organization seemed to be nothing more than a harmless group of patriotic Germans.

As the Bund continued to grow, however, and as Hitler's army began attacking other European nations, public opinion turned against Kuhn and his organization. Members of the American Legion, an organization of U.S. veterans of World War I, criticized the Bund. The U.S. Congress set up a House Un-American Activities Committee to investigate the Bund's ties to Germany. Major U.S. newspapers also began to investigate Kuhn

During the 1930s and 1940s, the Nazis had tried to "purify" the human race by murdering more than six million Jews, thousands of mentally retarded people, Gypsies, and others they believed were unfit to live.

and the other Bund leaders, and labor leaders threatened to close down Bund meetings by force.

In response to these attacks, the Bund members tried to make themselves appear more loyal to the United States and less interested in Germany. Kuhn replaced Nazi fighting songs with the "Star-Spangled Banner." The Bund began to display huge U.S. flags instead of swastikas at public rallies. When saluting, Kuhn replaced the words *Sieg Heil* (German for "Hail Victory") with the words "Free America."

On February 20, 1939, the Bund held a huge rally at Madison Square Garden in New York City to celebrate George Washington's birthday. The event, which attracted 20,000 people, celebrated Washington's belief that the United States should avoid permanent alliances with foreign nations and entanglements in their affairs. The Bund—as well as many Americans—wanted the United States to stay out of the coming conflict in Europe.

Aware of the dangers Hitler posed, hundreds of concerned Americans attend an anti-Nazi meeting during the late 1930s.

The rally at Madison Square Garden drew the attention of the press. Although the Bund had been trying to appear less sympathetic to Germany, this attempt failed as newspapers reported Bund speeches that glorified Hitler and published photos of swastikas and U.S. flags hanging side by side at the rally. Public opposition to the Bund grew, and investigations intensified.

The investigation led the U.S. attorney general to charge Kuhn with stealing money. Kuhn was found guilty and sentenced to prison. The Bund broke up into pro-Kuhn and anti-Kuhn factions, and membership dwindled. Some Bund leaders were loyal to Kuhn, while others turned against him. The organization lost thousands of members, as well as their membership dues.

As Hitler's tanks rolled across Europe in 1940 and 1941, Florida outlawed the Bund, and New Jersey closed a Bund camp. Wilhelm Kunze, the new leader of the Bund, took the organization underground. One day after the bombing of Pearl Harbor on December 7, 1941, the United States declared war on Japan. Within a week the United States also declared war on Germany and Italy. The leaders of the Bund disbanded the group.

In the meantime, future Nazi supporter George Lincoln Rockwell was fighting Nazi submarines in the Atlantic Ocean. Born on March 9, 1918, in Bloomington, Illinois, Rockwell was the son of a vaudeville and radio comedian. Rockwell had studied philosophy at Brown

University before joining the United States Navy in 1941. As a sailor, he reached the rank of lieutenant commander.

After the war ended in 1945, Rockwell struggled to earn a living as a commercial artist. But during the Korean War of the early 1950s, the navy recalled him to active duty. While in the military a second time, he read Hitler's book *Mein Kampf* (German for "My Struggle"), in which the Nazi leader explained his hatred for the Jewish people and other groups. Fascinated by Hitler's

Although the United States fought against Hitler's army in World War II, some Americans shared the Nazis' beliefs that whites with ancestors from northern Europe were superior to all other people.

philosophy and the white pride he preached, Rockwell became a convert to Nazism.

After leaving the military in 1954, Rockwell found that he could not adjust to the demands of steady work and civilian life. His failures, and a recurring dream in which he met Adolf Hitler, convinced him that his future lay with Nazism. By the late 1950s, he began planning a revival of the Nazi Party in the United States.

Rockwell formed a partnership with Harold Arrowsmith Jr., a wealthy businessman. Arrowsmith suspected that an international Jewish conspiracy was at work to control the world's commerce and government. To fight this conspiracy, Rockwell created the National Committee to Free America from Jewish Domination. To provide a headquarters for the organization, Arrowsmith invested in a house in Arlington, Virginia— located just outside of Washington, D.C.—where he also set up equipment to print his own articles about this alleged plot.

Rockwell, however, preferred direct action to writing. He took to the streets, leading noisy and sometimes violent rallies to denounce Jews, Communists, and anyone else he considered to be dangerous to the United States at that time. When the demonstrations drew widespread protests and criticism from the public, Arrowsmith withdrew from the organization and left Rockwell in charge of the Arlington headquarters.

In March 1959, Rockwell renamed his group the American Nazi Party. A keen organizer, Rockwell soon had Nazi cells operating in Dallas, Los Angeles, Chicago, Boston, and other major U.S. cities.

Most members of the American Nazi Party were young, working-class, white men who had trouble making their way in the world. Many were unemployed or had been in trouble with the law. Seeking an outlet for their frustrations, they turned against those groups they blamed for society's problems and for their own lack of opportunities. They saw Jewish people as sinister and greedy, and they resented racial minorities who were demanding the same rights and opportunities as white people. Upon joining the American Nazi Party, these young men swore an oath of loyalty to their comrades in the party and to the U.S. Constitution. They also pledged to admire Adolf Hitler and to obey the commands of George Lincoln Rockwell.

The American Nazi Party was a paramilitary organization, set up in the manner of the Bund or the German Nazi Party. Rockwell was the absolute leader of the group, and the men working under him held the military-style ranks of major, captain, or lieutenant. Each small group of storm troopers served under the command of a storm leader. Their uniforms consisted of a khaki shirt, trousers, swastika armbands, a narrow tie, and black boots. These outfits looked remarkably similar to those that had been worn by members of the Nazi Party in Germany during the World War II era. In addition to the regular uniforms, Rockwell and his leading officers also wore military-style ribbons over their left shirt pockets.

Rockwell prompted his storm troopers to speak out publicly against civil rights marchers, people who opposed the United States' involvement in the Vietnam War, and Jewish business owners. After selecting a highly visible location, Rockwell would stand at the center of a line of

Martin Luther King Jr. (front row, second from left) and other civil rights activists held nonviolent marches during the 1950s and 1960s to increase opportunities for minorities. Some whites, however, saw the civil rights movement as un-American.

followers and yell in an angry voice. Often, a confrontation would lead to a heated argument or even violence, with members of Rockwell's group and anti-Nazis attacking each other.

In Rockwell's opinion, modern civilization was in decline, and the people of the United States were growing lazy, soft, and spoiled. He praised Adolf Hitler as a leader who had tried to transform Europe, with Aryans dominating the world's economy, government, and culture.

Rockwell insisted that the Jews had conspired with President Franklin D. Roosevelt's administration and the Allies during World War II to defeat Hitler. Rockwell also claimed that the civil rights movement was an example of the international Jewish conspiracy in action.

At rallies organized by the American Nazi Party, Rockwell said that Jews were persuading black people to marry whites. He believed that interracial marriage would eventually lead the white race into extinction, as their children would be racially mixed. Rockwell concluded that whites and nonwhites would inevitably clash in a final worldwide conflict. He predicted that whites would win this conflict and dominate the world.

As people gathered to jeer when Rockwell spoke, the atmosphere grew tense between his followers and his enemies. Many of these demonstrations turned into fistfights or attacks with bottles and rocks. News coverage of the rallies gave valuable publicity to Rockwell's small organization.

In the summer of 1962, Rockwell traveled to England to meet with the British Nazi leader, Colin Jordan. Rockwell and Jordan worked together to write the Cotswold Agreement, which established the World Union of National Socialists. The agreement called for the group to create an international system of *apartheid*, which would divide the races by establishing separate governments for each race. Colin Jordan was named the worldwide Nazi leader. When the British government imprisoned Jordan because of his Nazi activities, this title passed to Rockwell.

The American Nazi Party, however, was suffering the same problems that the Bund had experienced in the 1920s. Membership was low, and the group's finances were poor. To raise money for his organization, Rockwell gave speeches at a number of large universities in the mid-1960s. The American Nazi Party also sold photographs of Hitler, pro-Nazi movies, tapes, calendars, and pamphlets, subscriptions to the *Stormtrooper* magazine—which carried Rockwell's own artwork—and copies of Rockwell's autobiography, *This Time the World*.

Despite Rockwell's efforts, the party never gained widespread support and never matched the membership numbers of the Bund. In 1965, Rockwell ran for governor of Virginia, promising to create an all-white, Christian state. His goal was to remove all Jews and blacks from Virginia by force and prevent them from returning to the state. On election day, Rockwell received only about

6,000 votes—a little more than one percent of the total votes cast.

At this time, the American Nazi Party was suffering from internal conflicts. When John Patler, an editor of the *Stormtrooper*, claimed that only blond-haired Aryans should belong to the American Nazi Party, a furious debate broke out within the ranks. Many Nazis had brown or black hair (as Hitler himself had)—and they felt just as loyal to the principles described by Rockwell and Hitler as Patler did. Rockwell began to regard Patler as a dangerous enemy. In March 1967, Rockwell reacted to this threat by throwing Patler out of the organization.

Patler responded by founding a rival organization called the American National Party. He also began publishing *Kill* magazine, in which he advised his followers to commit murder in the name of defending the Aryan race. Patler also felt a murderous rage toward Rockwell. Still angry about losing his American Nazi Party membership, Patler shot and killed Rockwell on the night of August 25, 1967, in the parking lot of an Arlington shopping center.

Without Rockwell's leadership, the American Nazi Party gradually lost the attention of the public. Rockwell's successor, a Nazi leader from Chicago named Matt Koehl, renamed the organization the National Socialist White People's Party. A new magazine, *White Power*, replaced the *Stormtrooper*. Koehl and his followers prepared for a racial war and the revolution that would place them in charge of a new United States government.

Years after George Lincoln Rockwell's death, members of other racist groups say they are merely promoting "white power," not hatred.

The legacy of Hitler and the Nazis of Germany still survives in the United States and in Europe. Some organizations devoted to Hitler's memory still exist in Germany. In many large cities, white teenagers who support the neo-Nazi movement shave their heads as a sign of their belief in white supremacy. Using Nazi slogans and salutes, these young "skinheads" sometimes attack racial minorities and immigrants.

In the United States, neo-Nazi groups include the Order and the White Aryan Resistance. But the Nazi supporters of the 1990s do not have a strong, charismatic leader to grab headlines and publicity. With the death of Rockwell, the Nazi movement in the United States now receives little attention, although many similar groups of violent, well-armed racists remain.

A charismatic speaker, Louis Farrakhan often draws thousands of listeners to hear his message of black separatism.

8

Louis Farrakhan
The Black Separatist

*T*he Great Depression of the 1930s brought despera-
tion and poverty to millions of people in the United
States. The Depression was especially difficult for the
black Americans who had moved from the South to work
in northern factories, but then lost their jobs during the
hard economic times. Seeking an answer to their problems and a glimmer of hope for their future, many of
them were anxious to hear the words of a peddler named
Wallace D. Fard.

Fard, who had adopted the name Wali Farrad Muhammad, was preaching a new message—a gospel based on the teachings of Islam. Founded in the seventh century A.D. by the Arab prophet Mohammad, Islam is based on the teachings of a holy book called the Koran. Followers of Islam are called Muslims (sometimes also spelled Moslems). They are devoted to the Koran and worship *Allah*, the word for God in Arabic. Fard offered his listeners a new interpretation of this ancient religion, an interpretation that seemed very relevant to their lives in the twentieth century.

Wali Farrad Muhammad believed that the members of the black race (which he called the ancient tribe of Shabazz) were Allah's chosen people. He also believed that all non-black races had been created in an experiment conducted by a scientist named Dr. Yacub, an outcast member of the Shabazz tribe. Ever since this evil deed, Fard explained, the white race had persecuted blacks.

Fard proclaimed that all white people were devils who were incapable of telling the truth and who were intent on enslaving blacks. He maintained that, although many white people called themselves Christians, whites refused to follow the teachings of Christianity. Fard predicted that the dominance of white people was about to end in a final battle between the races. He promised to reveal to black people the truth of their own past and to free them from their long and terrible oppression.

In the early 1930s, Fard spread his gospel through the streets of Detroit and in the private homes of his followers. After many of Fard's followers began giving him donations, he rented a lecture hall and named it the Temple of Islam. He also founded a school for children called the University of Islam.

Fard called his new sect the Nation of Islam. For his personal protection against anyone who might attack

Grade school students study at the University of Islam during the 1960s, about 30 years after the school was founded.

him, he trained a group of young guards that he called the Fruit of Islam. Fard's Nation of Islam slowly gathered strength in Detroit and several other cities.

In the summer of 1934, Fard disappeared. His followers did not know whether he had died or simply moved out of Detroit. Although Fard was gone, his vision was not forgotten. Fard had already named Elijah Poole, one of his closest advisers, as his successor. Like all members of the Nation of Islam, Elijah Poole dropped his "slave name"—the last name his ancestors had been given by their white masters—and adopted an Islamic surname (or last name). Now called Elijah Muhammad, he became the Nation of Islam's new leader.

Muhammad preached that blacks should begin preparing themselves for the upcoming racial battle that Fard had prophesied. They should not use alcohol and drugs, and they should never gamble. In addition, he said, they should hold steady jobs, never buy on credit, and always remain faithful to their spouses and children. Most importantly, they must separate themselves completely from the white world. Elijah Muhammad's ultimate goal was to establish a completely independent state for blacks in North America.

During the 1930s and 1940s, Elijah Muhammad attracted thousands of followers, who were known as Black Muslims. The message preached by Muhammad appealed to many who were angered by "white racism"— discrimination by white people against blacks. Many of

Until the 1860s, black people in the United States were legally bought and sold as property—losing their rights and much of their heritage. Since the early 1900s, many African Americans have tried to undo the legacy of slavery, in part by rejecting white society.

139

Elijah Muhammad (1897-1975), who became the leader of the Nation of Islam in 1934, called himself "the messenger of Allah." Muhammad told his many followers that God supported his plans for racial segregation.

Muhammad's followers found that sticking to the principles of the Nation of Islam improved their lives and their self-respect. The Nation soon expanded into the largest U.S. cities, including Chicago, New York, and Boston.

The Boston temple was under the direction of a young minister named Malcolm Little, who had converted to the faith while in a Boston jail in 1952. Like all members of the Nation of Islam, Little had dropped his last name. He now called himself Malcolm X.

During the 1960s, Malcolm X and the other Black Muslims took little interest in the growing civil rights movement that was demanding an equal place in society for black people. Instead, they insisted that blacks, no matter how hard they protested, would never win equal status and respect in the white-dominated United States. The Black Muslims believed that blacks would have to make their own world and their own freedoms, outside and separate from white society.

The Black Muslims set an example of separateness. They dressed in neat suits and bow ties, kept to a strict diet, and did not attend dances, sporting events, or movies. They allowed no whites into their temples and had as little communication as possible with what they saw as the "mainstream" society.

Another follower of Elijah Muhammad in Boston was Louis Eugene Walcott—later known as Louis Farrakhan. Born in 1933 in the Bronx section of New York City, Walcott had moved to Boston with his family when he was still a boy. A talent for music, acting, and public speaking made him popular in high school.

After graduation, Walcott studied at a teachers college in Winston-Salem, North Carolina. His real ambition, however, was to be a musician. He played the violin and once performed on "Ted Mack's Original Amateur Hour," a popular television variety show in the 1950s.

After college, he became a calypso artist and performed under the stage names "Calypso Gene" and "The Charmer."

Louis Walcott often visited the Nation of Islam temple in Boston and became a devoted Black Muslim. He adopted the name Louis X and began writing plays and songs inspired by his new beliefs. One of his plays, called *The Trial*, depicted a white man on trial for the crimes of his race. Near the end of the play, the white man was found guilty of all the crimes ever committed against African Americans. The character was then sentenced to death.

When Malcolm X left Boston to head the Nation of Islam congregation in Harlem, Louis X took over the Boston *mosque* (a Muslim house of worship). Changing his name again, Louis X became Louis Abdul Farrakhan. In the years to come, Farrakhan would become a leader in the national Black Muslim movement, widely respected for his energy, creativity, and powerful oratory.

Elijah Muhammad had been the undisputed leader of the Black Muslims since the 1930s. But in the 1960s, a scandal surrounding the leader split the Black Muslims into opposing factions. Rumors were spreading among Black Muslim leaders that Elijah Muhammad was breaking the tenets of the faith in his private life. Many of the leader's aides accused him of having sexual relations with several of his secretaries. When Malcolm X reported these rumors to his colleagues, Farrakhan defended Elijah Muhammad and turned against his former mentor, Malcolm X.

To reward Farrakhan for his loyalty, Elijah Muhammad made him the new leader of the New York City mosque. Malcolm X, meanwhile, left the United States in 1964 and went to Mecca, Saudi Arabia, a holy city in the Islamic religion. While in Mecca, Malcolm X became a follower of the Sunni branch of Islam, the sect that is followed by most of the world's Muslims.

When Malcolm X returned to the United States from his pilgrimage to Mecca, he brought back a new message for blacks. He now believed that a total separation of the races was not necessary. Malcolm X preached that blacks could cooperate with whites to some degree. Several Black Muslim leaders, including Louis Farrakhan, strongly condemned Malcolm X for his new beliefs and called him a traitor to their movement. Farrakhan himself announced that Malcolm X was "worthy of death."

Malcolm X paid a heavy price for his conversion. On February 21, 1965, just before making a speech, he was shot down on the stage of the Audubon Ballroom in Harlem. Three men, two of whom were Black Muslims, were later convicted of the crime. Many people, however, believed that the Central Intelligence Agency (CIA) was involved in the assassination or that a wider conspiracy against Malcolm X had existed among the Black

Muslim leadership. (As late as 1995, the controversy surrounding the death of Malcolm X remained in the news as the U.S. government accused one of Malcolm X's daughters, Qubilah Shabazz, of hiring an assassin to try to kill Farrakhan. Charges against Shabazz were dropped, however, when she agreed to undergo psychiatric counseling.)

After Malcolm X was assassinated, Elijah Muhammad designated Louis Farrakhan to be his spokesman. Ten years later, Elijah Muhammad died, leaving the Black Muslim movement in the hands of his son, Wallace Deen Muhammad. Like Malcolm X, W.D. Muhammad followed a more orthodox style of Islam. Rejecting the racial separatism preached by Wallace Fard in the early 1930s, W.D. Muhammad announced that white Muslims would be allowed to join the movement. He also renamed the Nation of Islam the World Community of Al-Islam. In 1980, the name was again changed, becoming the American Muslim Mission.

Farrakhan found himself at odds with the new leader of the Black Muslims. He believed the organization had lost its purpose, and he sought to uphold his uncompromising belief in racial separation. Farrakhan harshly criticized W.D. Muhammad and founded a new Nation of Islam to carry on the traditional teachings of Elijah Muhammad and Fard. Thousands of Black Muslims who had drifted away from the movement joined him.

Farrakhan operated his organization out of a mosque on the south side of Chicago. He preached strict adherence to the original codes of dress and behavior that were set down by Elijah Muhammad. Male members wore neat suits, while women wore long dresses and covered their heads.

Farrakhan set forth programs aimed to achieve total separation from whites and complete self-sufficiency for his followers. Instead of working within the large corporations that dominated the business world, he set up black-owned businesses that were created solely for the purpose of improving conditions for the members of the Nation of Islam. One of these businesses was known as POWER (short for People Organized to Work for Economic Rebirth). POWER products included soaps and lotions that were sold exclusively to black people.

By the early 1980s, Farrakhan had become one of the best-known black leaders in the country. His growing following among urban blacks was also drawing him into national politics. When civil rights leader Jesse Jackson ran for president in 1984, Farrakhan joined Jackson's campaign. The Jackson presidential campaign brought Farrakhan widespread exposure in the news media, but the close attention paid to his speeches and actions also brought controversy. Reporters noted that Farrakhan seemed to be intensifying the resentment that many African Americans felt toward Jewish people, many

*Civil rights spokesman the Reverend Jesse Jackson
(left), who has often preached on the virtues of racial
harmony, was harshly criticized during the 1980s for
supporting black separatist Louis Farrakhan.*

of whom operated shops in the black neighborhoods of inner cities.

In his campaign speeches in support of Jackson, Farrakhan accused the Jews of profiting at the expense of blacks in U.S. cities. Farrakhan also harshly criticized the Jewish nation of Israel for what he believed to be racist policies toward the Islamic Arabs living in that country and nearby. A Chicago newspaper quoted Farrakhan as saying that Judaism was a "gutter religion." Jewish leaders, in turn, accused the Nation of Islam and its leader of anti-Semitism.

Although Jesse Jackson lost the 1984 presidential election, Farrakhan continued his public speaking—and continued to draw attention as well as criticism. When the U.S. Senate voted to condemn him for his remarks, Farrakhan replied that Jews had too much influence in the U.S. government. When television stations and newspapers reported his harsh attacks on mainstream white society, Farrakhan accused the press of distorting his views and taking his comments out of context. He has said that white reporters and editors could not possibly understand what he or the Nation of Islam stood for.

When he spoke in public auditoriums and on college campuses during the 1980s, Farrakhan attracted thousands of listeners. In his speeches, he continued to criticize Jews, as well as white people in general. Farrakhan also spoke out against blacks who were trying to assimilate into middle-class society. He would note the spread of poverty, drug addiction, and unemployment in cities throughout the United States, and then say that white leaders were working together to impoverish blacks, making them weak and dependent.

Farrakhan also saw a conspiracy behind the spread of the deadly AIDS virus. According to this theory, AIDS (Acquired Immune Deficiency Syndrome) was part of a secret plan to wipe out the world's black population. Rumors spread by word of mouth and in the black press that white scientists had deliberately created the virus and let it loose among the people of Africa, from where it eventually spread to the United States. This conspiracy theory reminded some people of the original teachings of W. D. Fard, who had claimed that an evil scientist had created the white race.

While not everyone believed Farrakhan's AIDS theories, many people thought he was telling the truth about race relations in the United States. Moreover, the harsh criticism Farrakhan received from the mainstream press because of his attacks on Jews only served to strengthen his support. Seeking an explanation for the economic and social problems of their community, many blacks supported Farrakhan merely because so many powerful people seemed to oppose him. At least, they thought, the Nation of Islam shared with them a common enemy—white society.

Loyalty to Farrakhan has been strengthened over the past few years by the good deeds of the Nation of

Islam. Under Farrakhan's guidance, the Nation has converted and helped to reform thousands of criminals. A Nation of Islam program known as Dopebusters has also worked to rid a poor neighborhood in Washington, D.C. of drug dealers. Many people—both black and white—support these constructive actions and excuse Farrakhan's extreme ideas as unimportant to his overall message.

In a nation that is still struggling with race relations, Louis Farrakhan's words have found thousands of eager listeners. As a result, the division of the races preached years ago by W. D. Fard and Elijah Muhammad has remained a central idea of the Nation of Islam. At the same time, the economic and social problems of black people in the United States are worsening—giving many people more reason to support the message of Louis Farrakhan.

Not everyone is convinced that Farrakhan or other controversial figures really are demagogues. Many people would argue that some level of hatemongering is necessary to energize any cultural or political movement. Nevertheless, history has been filled with intolerant people who distorted the truth or deliberately harmed others under the guise of good intentions.

Bibliography

Anderson, Jack, and Ronald W. May. *McCarthy: The Man, The Senator, The "ism."* Boston: Beacon Press, 1952.

Bell, Leland V. *In Hitler's Shadow: The Anatomy of American Nazism.* Port Washington: Kennikat Press, 1973.

Chalmers, David M. *Hooded Americanism: The History of the Ku Klux Klan.* New York: Franklin Watts, 1981.

Coleman, Kenneth, ed. *A History of Georgia.* Athens: University of Georgia Press, 1977.

Cook, Fred J. *The Demagogues.* New York: Macmillan, 1972.

——————. *The Ku Klux Klan: America's Recurring Nightmare.* Englewood Cliffs, N.J.: Messner, 1989.

——————. *The Nightmare Decade: The Life and Times of Senator Joe McCarthy.* New York: Random House, 1971.

Corry, John. "Howard's End." *The American Spectator,* April/May 1994.

"Farrakhan." *National Review,* April 4, 1994.

Gragg, Larry. *A Quest for Security: The Life of Samuel Parris, 1653-1720.* Westport, Conn.: Greenwood Press, 1990.

Hansen, Chadwick. *Witchcraft at Salem.* New York: Braziller, 1969.

Henry, Stuart C. *Unvanquished Puritan: A Portrait of Lyman Beecher.* Grand Rapids: William B. Eerdmans, 1973.

Lincoln, C. Eric. *The Black Muslims in America.* Grand Rapids: William B. Eerdmans, 1994.

"Louis Farrakhan." *Current Biography Yearbook, 1992.*

Marcus, Sheldon. *Father Coughlin: The Tumultuous Life of the Priest of the Little Flower.* Boston: Little, Brown and Company, 1973.

Martin, Harold H. *Georgia: A Bicentennial History.* New York: W. W. Norton, 1977.

Reed, Adolph, Jr. "False Prophet." *The Nation,* January 21-28, 1991.

Woodward, C. Vann. *Tom Watson, Agrarian Rebel.* New York: Oxford University Press, 1938.

Index

abolitionists, 38, 43

AIDS (Acquired Immune Deficiency Syndrome), 148

American Legion, 58, 121

American Muslim Mission, 144

American Nazi Party, 8, 116, 127-131; conflicts within, 131

anti-Communism, 103-104, 105, 109

apartheid, 130

Army-McCarthy hearings, 111, 113-114

Arrowsmith, Harold Jr., 126

Aryans, 120, 129, 131

atheists, 29, 35

Barbados, 12, 25

Beecher, Catherine, 42

Beecher, David, 28

Beecher, Henry Ward, 42

Beecher, Lyman, 8, 26; anti-Catholic attitude of, 35-37, 39; belief of, in Calvinist doctrine, 31, 33; children of, 32, 42-43; death of, 43; early years of, 28-29; as minister, 31-34; as pastor of Congregationalist church in Boston, 34-35, 37-38; as president of Lane Theological Seminary, 38, 39-42; at

Yale College, 28-29, 31

Bethany: A Story of the Old South, 53

Bible, 20, 28, 33

Birmingham, Alabama, church bombing in, 76-77

Birth of a Nation, 66

Bishop, Bridget, 20

Black, James, 49-50, 51

blacklisting, 105

black magic, 16

Black Muslims, 9, 138, 141, 142, 143, 144. *See also* Nation of Islam

blacks: attacks on, 50, 51, 54-55, 65, 77; attitudes toward, 54, 55, 56, 62, 65, 66, 68, 75, 118, 129, 130-131, 138; and Ku Klux Klan, 65, 69, 70, 78, 79; and Nation of Islam, 137-138, 141, 143, 145, 148; rights of, 55, 79, 117; separatism movement among, 9, 134, 138, 141, 143, 144, 145, 149

Bonaparte, Napoleon, 52

Browder, Earl, 109

Bryan, William Jennings, 51, 52, 53

Buell, Samuel, 31

Bund, German-American, 75, 120-124, 127, 130

Butler, John Marshall, 109

155

156

ABOUT THE AUTHOR

TOM STREISSGUTH was born in Washington, D.C., in 1958, and is a graduate of Yale University. He has traveled widely in Europe and the Middle East, and has worked as a teacher, editor, and journalist. Streissguth is also the author of *Soviet Leaders from Lenin to Gorbachev*, *International Terrorists*, *Hoaxers and Hustlers*, and *Charismatic Cult Leaders*. He lives in Minneapolis with his wife and two daughters.

Photo Credits

Photographs courtesy of: Georgia Department of Archives and History, pp. 6, 57 (top), 59, 67; Library of Congress, pp. 8, 14, 18, 21, 22, 24, 32, 36, 40, 41, 43, 44, 51, 53, 57 (bottom), 63, 74, 76, 82, 84, 87, 98, 112, 122, 139; Massachusetts Historical Society, p. 10; Ohio Historical Society, pp. 26, 39; Yale University Library, pp. 29, 30; Wide World Photos, p. 60; Tennessee State Library and Archives, p. 64; Special Collections, Michigan State University Libraries, p. 72; Louisiana State Archives, p. 78; Chicago Historical Society, p. 79; Detroit Public Library, pp. 80, 85; Franklin D. Roosevelt Library, p. 90; Minnesota Historical Society, pp. 95, 123; National Archives, pp. 103, 104 (both), 119, 128; Northwood Institute Margaret Chase Smith Library, p. 107; The Bettmann Archive, pp. 108, 111, 116, 132, 134, 137, 140, 146; and Simon Wiesenthal Center, Beit Ha Shoah Museum, p. 125.